MW01179208

Messiah Is Coming

By Mark Jeske

TIME OF
GRACE®
WITH PASTOR MARK JESKE

xulon
PRESS

Copyright © 2011 by Time of Grace Ministry

Messiah Is Coming
by Mark Jeske

Printed in the United States of America

ISBN 9781619042551

All rights reserved solely by the copyright holder. The copyright holder guarantees all contents are original and do not infringe upon the legal rights of any other person or work. No part of this book may be reproduced in any form without the permission of the copyright holder. The views expressed in this book are not necessarily those of the publisher.

Unless otherwise indicated, Bible quotations are taken from The HOLY BIBLE, NEW INTERNATIONAL VERSION®. NIV®. Copyright © 1973, 1978, 1984 by Biblica, Inc.™ Used by permission of Zondervan.

Time of Grace Ministry
P.O. Box 301, Milwaukee, WI 53201-0301
414.562.8463 or 1.800.661.3311
info@timeofgrace.org
www.timeofgrace.org

www.xulonpress.com

With a grateful and humble heart, I would like to dedicate this little volume to three patient, wonderful women who take my sometimes confusing and convoluted rants and edit them into something you might find helpful and interesting. To Linda Buxa, Adrea Knoll, and Amanda Swiontek—my sincerest thanks.

Contents

Introduction ix

Chapter 1 11
Who Will He Be?

Chapter 2 33
What Kind of Welcome Does He Deserve?

Chapter 3 59
Where Will He Come From?

Chapter 4 79
What Did He Come to Do?

Chapter 5 105
Christ Is Born—So What?

Chapter 6 .... **117**

The Bonus Chapter

Study Guides **127**

Introduction

Who of us has never had a broken heart? Do you know anybody whose hopes have never been dashed? Who of us has escaped frustration, loss, pain, and defeat in life?

The evil one interprets those hardships for you and suggests that your God is careless, cruel, impotent, absent, or never existed in the first place. He either flatters you into thinking you can make your own way or mocks you for being such a loser. The more we listen to his lies, the greater the gloom that settles on our hearts.

But Messiah is coming! The first coming of Jesus Christ to earth demonstrated that God keeps his promises. That he cared enough to come in person. That he was willing to empty himself to make us full. That purchasing forgiveness for our sins was more important than his own comfort or life. That God always wins in the end.

And Messiah is coming again. That bright hope keeps us going forward even when we drag heavy weights. That bright promise means that evil and pain and suffering and even death are only temporary. What is permanent is our relationship with a God who loves us freely and unconditionally and whose divine heart beats with urgency to bring you home, to his Home.

Messiah Is Coming explores some of God's most wonderful prophetic Scriptures, which over the millennia have given hope and new strength to many struggling believers. May God's words and promises give hope and strength to you too.

Chapter 1

Who Will He Be?

December 7, 1941, is one of the most miserable days in the history of the United States. President Franklin D. Roosevelt called it a "date which will live in infamy." Americans were caught by surprise as the Japanese Air Force bombed and strafed the Pacific fleet at anchor in Pearl Harbor and yanked the United States into World War II. That same day the Japanese also launched an assault on Malaysia. The goal was to reach the seemingly impregnable British fortress in Singapore, which was surrounded on three sides by water and bordered on the other by dense jungle. With such a protected location and huge guns facing the sea, the soldiers stationed in Singapore believed no attack would be launched against the "Gibraltar of the East." Oh, were they wrong.

To Britain's great shock, the Japanese did not assault Singapore by sea. Instead, they landed miles and miles up the peninsula. They moved ground troops through the jungle with light tanks and bicycles and finally encircled the fortress at Singapore. Though the British troops outnumbered the Japanese more than three to one—130,000 men to Japan's 30,000—they were badly outmaneuvered, and the day came when the commanders realized that they would have to surrender. The troops and civilians in Singapore could do nothing more than wait and wonder if they would be killed during the invasion or taken captive.

Rewind two thousand years. The people of Jerusalem were facing the same situation, dreading their impending defeat. They were undergoing a land assault from the north. As they watched their lines of defense being broken down one by one, their capital was surely doomed. It was at this time of maximum stress that God said, "I know things look really— *really*—bad right now, but hang in there: Messiah is coming. Soon enough, at the time I choose, a virgin will give birth to a son and will '*give him the name Jesus. He will be great and will be called the Son of the Most High. The Lord God will give him the throne of his father David, and he will reign over the house of Jacob forever; his kingdom will never end'"* (Luke 1:31-33).

That promised Messiah changed everything. Even in the face of near-certain military defeat, the Israelites also anticipated God's promised world-changing, life-changing event. Who is this champion? Who will he be? Through the prophet Isaiah, God gave them the answer—and so much more. As God told the people what his plans were, what was going on in his mind and heart, he showed that he is a God of both law and gospel, a God of judgment and mercy, a God of accountability and a God of unwavering love. From God's point of view, the military invasion was a small problem, easily solved. Defeated armies, lost wealth, shrunken power—small problems all. He could replace those things in the snap of his fingers. What really mattered to God was whether or not people would believe in his promise of a Messiah.

Can you relate to the Israelites? Christmastime is supposed to be a time of joy, anticipation, and magic. Everything is supposed to work out. Hopes of love and togetherness and prosperity are supposed to come true. But there are hard realities in December too. Have hardships and personal setbacks made you anxious, pessimistic, and bitter? Can Israel's promised

13

Messiah be your Savior too? Do you know who this Messiah is? Do you believe what God says about him?

In the 700s B.C., the once-proud united kingdom of David and Solomon had split in half. Israel was the northern kingdom; the small southern kingdom was called Judah. They had battled each other for years, but this time it looked as though little Judah, with its capital at Jerusalem, was going under for good. The northern king of Israel, a thug by the name of Pekah, had persuaded King Rezin of Aram—what we call Syria today—to join him in a military alliance. They would invade Judah and smash Jerusalem to pieces. So far, the plan was working brilliantly. They had crushed an army of 120,000 soldiers from Judah, and badly weakened Jerusalem was in their sights.

Leading the people of Judah was King Ahaz, who was working overtime to become one of the worst kings the southern nation ever had. Ahaz had had so little respect for the God of his ancestor David that he closed the temple in Jerusalem and stopped all the worship and sacrifices. Instead, he had altars built to heathen gods and went so far as to sacrifice one of his own children, imitating the horrible customs of the Canaanite religions around him. I would have completely understood (probably even approved) if at this time the Bible had recorded: "Because of Ahaz' wicked deeds, the Lord caused the earth to open and swallow Ahaz and his entire family. Then he placed a faithful king on the throne."

Instead, it was at this moment God decided to be patient with Ahaz and the people of Judah and to give them extraordinary blessings even while they were at a sickeningly low point, morally and spiritually. As God watched the war carefully and set its limits, he saw Ahaz' panic and thought, "Perfect! I've got something to tell you, Ahaz, and right now you're probably ready to hear it. I'm going to show you some mercy in hopes that you will come back to me."

With that background, we are ready to dive in and join the story in Isaiah chapter 7. Let me warn you, this is not your typical Christmas preparation. In fact, this story will get heavy and depressing before it gets better. My guess, though, is that you know heaviness too, and you may well identify with the Israelites' struggle more than with happy lights or music or parties, which are designed to give others the impression that all is right in the world. Maybe not all is right in your world right now.

King Rezin of Aram and Pekah son of Remaliah king of Israel marched up to fight against Jerusalem, but they could not overpower it.

Now the house of David was told, "Aram has allied itself with Ephraim"; so the hearts of Ahaz and his people were shaken, as the trees of the forest are shaken by the wind.

Then the Lord said to Isaiah, "Go out, you and your son Shear-Jashub, to meet Ahaz at the end of the aqueduct of the Upper Pool, on the road to the Washerman's Field. Say to him, 'Be careful, keep calm and don't be afraid. Do not lose heart because of these two smoldering stubs of fire-wood—because of the fierce anger of Rezin and Aram and of the son of Remaliah. Aram, Ephraim and Remaliah's son have plotted your ruin, saying, "Let us invade Judah; let us tear it apart and divide it among ourselves, and make the son of Tabeel king over it."'" (Isaiah 7:1-6)

The residents of Jerusalem could look over the city walls and see that Rezin and Pekah had slowed down but were still planning to crush Jerusalem and kill or enslave them. Even though the house of David, the royal dynasty of the southern kingdom, was shaking in its sandals, the people were not going to give up without a fight against Ephraim (i.e., the northern kingdom).

The Lord stepped in and gave Isaiah a message: "Take your son and go meet this evil king who has not followed a single one of my commands." Forgive me, but I cannot let Isaiah's son's name slide by without a comment. Isaiah had two boys with two very different names. One got the "bad-news" name: Maher-Shalal-Hash-Baz means "one who is eager for the spoils." The other, Shear-Jashub, got a name of hope. In Hebrew it means "a remnant will return." So when Isaiah went to meet Ahaz, he took along the son whose very name reminded the people that a remnant, a small piece, of the nation would live on and flourish in the future. With his son standing next to him, Isaiah told Ahaz to keep calm and urged him not to be afraid—even though God had heard Pekah and Rezin plotting about how they were going to crush Judah, kill the royal family, and seize control of the country.

Ahaz' guilty conscience may have led him to expect harsh condemnation from the God he had been insulting. But, in fact, Isaiah's message was full of hope:

"Yet this is what the Sovereign LORD says:

'It will not take place, it will not happen, for the head of Aram is Damascus, and the head of Damascus is only Rezin. Within sixty-five years Ephraim will be too shattered to be a people. The head of Ephraim is Samaria, and the head of Samaria is only Remaliah's son. If you do not stand firm in your faith, you will not stand at all.'"

Again the LORD spoke to Ahaz, "Ask the LORD your God for a sign, whether in the deepest depths or in the highest heights."

But Ahaz said, "I will not ask; I will not put the LORD to the test." (Isaiah 7:7-12)

As far as Ahaz could see, there was nothing but disaster coming. But God had a different view, and he patiently shared it with Ahaz. "Rezin is only a man—and he's only the king of an earthly country. And you're scared of Pekah? Well, no worries, he's simply a man too—and his country will be shattered within the next 65 years." As it turned out, both Rezin and Pekah died within 3 years, and the northern kingdom fell in only 14. After reminding Ahaz that he had the war handled, God had another message. "I am your defense. If you have me on your side, you can lick the world. If you don't have me, then you should be terrified. But you do have me! Have faith in me. Listen to my words. Let me explain the drama that you're in right now. Listen! Let me tell you how things are going to be."

In a jaw-dropping, boneheaded move, Ahaz did not take God's first message to heart. This is another time where I would have expected God to squash Ahaz like a bug, simply to be done with him. But he didn't. God, who does not seem to have a three-strikes policy, showed this evil king even *more* patience.

"I'm going to give you something I hardly ever give," said God. "I'm giving you the chance to design a test. Ask me to do something miraculous. I'll even break all the laws of nature just to demonstrate these prophecies are true."

Do you know how many people all over the world from the beginning of time have wanted this opportunity? Admit it with me; you have thought about what your three wishes would be if you found a genie's lamp. And now, the God of the whole entire universe, who set the stars in the sky, was giving Ahaz the dream of a lifetime.

So what did Ahaz do? He said, "Thanks, but no thanks."

I can almost hear Isaiah say, "Are you kidding me?" Note how in the beginning of this section Isaiah told Ahaz to "ask the LORD *your* God . . ." but by the end he asked, "Will you try the patience of *my* God?" Isaiah sadly realized that Ahaz did not believe in Israel's God at all. Still, this was not about Ahaz. It was about God and his plan to keep all his promises, which is why he decided to give a sign anyway, whether Ahaz wanted one or not.

> *Then Isaiah said, "Hear now, you house of David! Is it not enough to try the patience of men? Will you try the patience of my God also? Therefore the Lord himself will give you a sign: The virgin will be with child and will give birth to a son, and will call him Immanuel. He will*

eat curds and honey when he knows enough to reject the wrong and choose the right. But before the boy knows enough to reject the wrong and choose the right, the land of the two kings you dread will be laid waste. The Lord *will bring on you and on your people and on the house of your father a time unlike any since Ephraim broke away from Judah—he will bring the king of Assyria."* (Isaiah 7:13-17)

Now, in the middle of Israel's gloom, in the middle of your sadness and struggles, we finally get to the good news! God gave a sign that broke all the laws of nature and showed his kindly intent toward the people of the world: *"The virgin will be with child and will give birth to a son, and will call him Immanuel."* In the middle of a disastrous civil war, with an evil king who didn't want a sign, God stepped in and gave two extraordinary prophecies about the Messiah. One, a *virgin* would conceive. From the body of this young, unmarried, virgin woman, Jesus would be born. You can barely get your mind around that idea when the second prophecy comes. His mother would name him "God with us" (Immanuel). Almighty, eternal God was going to rescue his planet *in person.*

Even if Ahaz had accepted God's offer to perform any sign he asked for, his limited human brain would never have stretched this far. A pregnant virgin? Only God could come up with that one—and the only God did! Through his almighty power, God the Holy Spirit provided the equivalent of what the male sperm cell normally does in fertilizing an egg. When Immanuel was born, he was the son of a woman without an earthly father and the Son of a heavenly Father with no heavenly mother

You may have a hard time believing that that is possible. Yet when the angel Gabriel came to Mary, he told her, "Mary, you are going to become pregnant, but not with the assistance of any other male. It will be through the power of the Holy Spirit. I know you're a virgin. God can do it. Believe me. God can do anything. Your child is going to be three kinds of son. He is going to be the son of you, the son of David (the inheritor of the royal line of the Jewish kings of Israel), and the Son of God. God's Son will be in your own insides, Mary." She believed that unbelievable message (see Luke 1:26-38).

Nine months after Gabriel's visit, the second part of the prophecy was fulfilled. Immanuel was born. God (in the Hebrew language *El*) was with us (in

Hebrew *immanu).* That incomprehensible concept is the way God chose to personally rescue us from our worst nightmare. Hebrews 2:14 puts it this way: *"Since the children have flesh and blood, he too shared in their humanity."* That is extraordinary. He came to this world not to be merely human-like or human-ish. He came not merely to be like us, but to *be* us, fully human in every way yet still fully God. He didn't come into the world as Adam did, as an adult male. His life trajectory was the same as yours. He spent nine months in Mary's womb. He went through the birth process only to be born in a dark, unsanitary barn amid the mooing and the braying and the baaing of animals. He had a real heart to pump the real blood in his real veins. He had to learn to talk and walk, he had to be potty trained and weaned, and he needed to learn how to say please and thank you. He also had to learn the spiritual things. He had to go to synagogue school and memorize Bible passages one by one, the way I did as a child.

As he got older, it did not get easier. His carpenter stepfather, Joseph, probably taught young Jesus how to be a carpenter too. He who made the earth had to learn how to build a table. He who fills the universe had to walk wherever he went. He who sustains the universe with his mighty strength fell tired into his bed (or cot or mat or front of a boat) each night. The God who feeds the universe had to eat three times a day to fuel his machine. These are mind-boggling contradictions, aren't they?

I still can't get over it, and I hope you can't either. Christ loves us so much that he chose to put himself through that. He became human like us—and for us—all so he could fight Satan as a human being. I can tell you that this is not how my plan to save the world would have looked. I always used to think when I was a kid, "God should just kill the devil. Get it over with, and we'll all be happy." Well, now that I am older, I know that killing the devil is, first of all, way too easy a way out for Satan. He deserves to suffer for all the pain and suffering he has caused in the world. Second, killing the devil does nothing to help you, because you have been infected and are now a miniature devil yourself. If your daughter caught the flu, you would not ask the principal to expel the child who infected her. You know that kicking out the source of the infection does not make your child healthy again.

God knows that too. He knew we needed a rescue that couldn't be accomplished by just incinerating Satan. God's brilliant plan was based completely on another human being, one who was God himself, coming to be born into our world, to be our personal substitute, a fully human substitute. In our place he kept all of the commandments. He reenacted Adam and Eve's temptation, only this time he said no to the devil and did it again and again and again. Every day he lived, he fought with Satan on your and my behalf, in our place, as a human, with flesh and blood just like ours. Every day of your life you have a sympathetic friend in heaven who advocates for you, since he knows our human struggle.

Immanuel, Jesus Christ, brought the fullness of God to earth in human form and joined together a divine and human nature. Immanuel, God and man in human form, has come to pronounce forgiveness and pardon upon us.

What war is raging in your life right now? Do you feel the enemy stalking you through the jungle? Can you see the lines of your defense falling one by one? Let the news of Immanuel bring you peace right now.

Maybe your job is grinding you down. Maybe you wish you had a job so the financial worries hanging over your head would not seem quite so menacing. Perhaps you are in your own civil war. Do the relationships in your life leave you wounded and bleeding? Maybe you are in a marriage where every day is simply a day to survive, not to thrive. Or is a lack of a relationship your struggle? Does loneliness dog you?

Are you waging an internal war? Do you dislike or maybe even hate yourself? Is your physical body weary, breaking down? Maybe addiction, pain, and illness rob your strength.

Just as that Messiah-promise was life and death to Ahaz, it is life and death to you and me as well. Because of the evil and sin within all people, all of planet Earth—including Singapore, Jerusalem, and your town—was and is headed into major trouble with God. No person on earth can do a single thing to stop it. Just as Isaiah's message to Ahaz started with bad news, his message for you does too.

So justice is far from us, and righteousness does not reach us. We look for light, but all is darkness; for brightness, but we walk in deep shadows. Like the blind we grope along the wall, feeling our way like men without eyes. At midday we stumble as if it were twilight; among the strong, we are like the dead. We all growl like bears; we moan mournfully like doves. We look for justice, but find none; for deliverance, but it is far away. (Isaiah 59:9-11)

Maybe you feel the same way. The people in your life whom you had trusted turn out instead to embrace injustice. So many things about your life don't seem fair, and you can't change them. To offset their disappointment, people look for something, anything, to fill the emptiness, but they can't find it because we all *"walk in deep shadows."* We look in the wrong places for fulfillment. The Israelites chased after Baal. Today people try every Zen philosophy or New Age gimmick, looking for spiritual light and revelation. If spirituality doesn't fix it, we might give the worldly options a try. Chasing money, sexual freedom, and quick chemical highs may distract us for a few moments. But they don't satisfy. They don't give truth and light and wisdom, only slavery and brokenness. Isaiah knew it and we do too. We want to be smart, but we know we are often fools. We know we are weak, so in our insecurity we growl at one another. We let our tempers fly. We moan on the phone to our friends and complain to anyone who will listen about our situation. Even when we think we see a light at the end of the tunnel, we fear it's probably just an approaching train.

> *For our offenses are many in your sight, and our sins testify against us. Our offenses are ever with us, and we acknowledge our iniquities: rebellion and treachery against the LORD, turning our backs on our God, fomenting oppression and revolt, uttering lies our hearts have conceived. So justice is driven back, and righteousness stands at a distance; truth has stumbled in the streets, honesty cannot enter. Truth is nowhere to be found, and whoever shuns evil becomes a prey.* (Isaiah 59:12-15)

Isaiah pretty much tells it like it is, isn't it so? I don't want to hear this any more than the Israelites did. It is tempting to lay blame on everyone else, as if we have no control over our situations. We are fooling ourselves if we believe that. In reality, we have been trying to control everything ourselves. We have lost our way because we have not been paying attention to God. The darkness is real, and Isaiah lays it out in this verse: *"Our offenses are many in your sight."* Just like the people of God in the eighth century B.C., we have plenty of reasons to be gloomy, especially when we look at ourselves and see that much of our pain is self-inflicted. Further, you and I have to admit that we have contributed to the pain of the people around us. All of us—young and old, men, women, teens, and children—know how to be cruel, jealous, petty, boastful, selfish, and abusive.

Do these admissions make you want to slam this book down and walk away, wondering why you ever bothered to pick it up? Seriously—if you had wanted bad news, you could have read a newspaper. But don't run away. Stick with me for just a bit. God isn't done speaking. Isaiah's words must have caused the same gloomy thoughts among the Israelite people. For them, it must really have looked as though darkness was over everything. Their nation was under attack; their national economy was in a shambles; their national and personal futures seemed bleak. I'm sure they now considered God's term "chosen nation" for them with only bitterness. Under it all lay guilt. They knew Isaiah was right—their troubles were their own doing.

At just the right time, God gave Isaiah another good-news message to share with his people. It's a good-news message for everybody who is gloomy; everybody who is depressed; everybody who struggles;

everybody who has a load of frustration; everybody who has regrets, guilt, fears, and unfulfilled hopes and longings. Listen to this:

> *"Arise, shine, for your light has come, and the glory of the LORD rises upon you. See, darkness covers the earth and thick darkness is over the peoples, but the LORD rises upon you and his glory appears over you."* (Isaiah 60:1,2)

Are you still curled up in the fetal position from the bad news we just read together? Well, get up—arise! This is for you, for people who are cringing, who are hiding, who are moping, who are grieving, who are exhausted at nine o'clock in the morning, whose reserves are gone, and whose needle is on empty. There is good news here for you. Get up; look up, because the light has come, the light of the One who will be born of a virgin. What I love about this passage is that Mary was not going to conceive her baby for another seven hundred years. You would think Isaiah should have said, "Your light *will* come; the glory of the Lord *will* rise upon you." Instead, God's spokesman used the past tense; he said the light *has* come. He was talking about the Messiah—the one promised to King

Ahaz just 53 chapters ago, who had not come yet. It does not make sense to our limited way of viewing time. But it works when you are the God who invented time, who transcends time, who lives simultaneously in the past and future. When God chooses to reveal an event that is "future" to us, he can simply announce a fact, a done deal, past tense, because he is already an eyewitness to something that already happened. In fact, for God everything in a sense is past tense.

Yet the Israelites still had to live through their hard present. When Isaiah said, *"Your light has come,"* it still looked dark in 730 B.C., and it was getting darker. Their brightest hope, the presence of the *"glory of the Lord"* (i.e., the bright cloud that lived in the inner sanctuary of the temple, hovering over the golden box, the ark of the covenant) was going to leave them. That bright cloud was the sign of the presence of God on the earth, but even with God in the middle of them, the Israelites found the worship of other gods exciting and fulfilling. Soon God would allow opposing armies to break in and destroy the temple. They would tear down the veiling curtain and carry off the ark; the glory would vanish.

But Isaiah was allowed to see that the glory would come back. The discipline of the captivity would do its hard work, the people would repent, and the nation would be reconstituted. At just the right time, just as God had promised, a Savior was born in Israel. He is the light-bringer. His birth guarantees that there is hope for all who trust in him. His birth guarantees that God still loves the human race. His birth guarantees that Satan hasn't won after all. His birth guarantees that God's plans march steadily forward, even when they take centuries to develop and unfold.

When you feel misery and hopelessness and darkness hovering over you like a gray cloud, imagine standing next to the little manger that holds the Son of God. Imagine glorious light streaming out of that rude cradle-bed. That light shines on you. Let God's words and God's promises drive the gloom from your heart. You are loved! You are forgiven! You are somebody! You are immortal!

Chapter 2

What Kind of Welcome Does He Deserve?

If you are a trivia buff, you probably know that "Happy Birthday to You" is the most popular song in the world. And with good reason! First published in a songbook in 1893, the tune was called "Good Morning to All" and was written by Patty and Mildred Hill, two kindergarten teachers who happened to be sisters. The further development is in dispute, but somewhere along the line, someone added the lyrics "happy birthday to you" to the tune and copyrighted it. Now any time it is used in the movies, in sheet music, or in any commercial use, companies have to pay. Until 2030, when the song becomes public domain, the current copyright owners, Time Warner, make about $5,000 a day in royalties off of that one little song.

By some bit of song magic, that dorky little tune is now so wedded to the concept of having a birthday celebration that you cannot have a satisfactory birthday unless people sing it to you at some point during the day. The same goes for cake. I would not mind a worldwide custom of birthday donuts, but apparently it has to be cake—maybe because you can write "Happy Birthday" on top of it in frosting cursive. So if you have not heard the song and you have not had a cake with candles on it denoting roughly how old you are, you apparently cannot really say you have celebrated your birthday. And don't forget the presents. At some point in history, someone decided there had to be an exchange of products for you to have a true birthday. So make your list of the birthday trifecta: song, cake, presents. Once you check off those boxes, you can rest easy that you still have friends and that your life has been validated.

Well, Christmas is the biggest birthday celebration I know of, but I am fairly certain that this incredible birthday boy is not going to get a song, cake, or wrapped packages. But what if you wanted to have a significant birthday celebration for him? How can you prepare and organize a reception for this baby, the Messiah, whose virgin birth was revealed to King Ahaz? The Bible has a great story to share that helps us get ready to give Jesus the reception and welcome that he deserves, simply because of who he is. The greatest honor you can give the Messiah is to believe who he says he is, believe he really did what he said he came to do, and believe that all of his promises to you will really come true.

This story is not from Jesus' birth accounts in Scripture but took place actually *after* the Christmas account. In this amazing story, some Parthian nobility—you may know them better as the Magi, or "wise men"—show us the appropriate way to celebrate Jesus' birth.

After Jesus was born in Bethlehem in Judea, during the time of King Herod, Magi from the east came to Jerusalem and asked, "Where is the one who has been born king of the Jews? We saw his star in the east and have come to worship him."

When King Herod heard this he was disturbed, and all Jerusalem with him. When he had called together all the people's chief priests and teachers of the law, he asked them where the Christ was to be born. "In Bethlehem in Judea," they replied, "for this is what the prophet has written:

"'But you, Bethlehem, in the land of Judah, are by no means least among the rulers of Judah; for out of you will come a ruler who will be the shephord of my pcoplc Israel.'"

Then Herod called the Magi secretly and found out from them the exact time the star had appeared. He sent them to Bethlehem and said, "Go and make a careful search for the child. As soon as you find him, report to me, so that I too may go and worship him." (Matthew 2:1-8)

Of the four Herods mentioned in the New Testament, this one, also known as Herod the Great, is the first of them—and the worst of them. No one would ever have dreamed of calling him "Herod the Good" because he was a violent pig of a man. Not a natural born king, he seized power, essentially in a coup, and allied himself with the Roman Empire. Though just a governor, accountable to the Roman Caesar, he wanted to be called a king, and the Romans humored him with the title on the assumption that then the restive Jewish population could pretend that they were still at least partially independent. Like most tyrants, Herod was paranoid and suspicious of everyone whom he thought might be a threat—he even killed his own children when he suspected they were trying to supplant him.

By the time Jesus was born, Herod had been ruling for 40 years and was near the end of his life. But his cunning and instincts for self-preservation were still sharp, and he was looking out not only for himself but for his dynasty. These Magi, visitors who came to town looking for the one born king of the Jews, were Parthians—today we might call them Iranians. His grudge against these people went back to the beginning of his reign. He had been ruling for only a couple of years when, during a key battle between the Romans and the Parthians, the Romans had to retreat and Herod was driven from his throne. He fled for his life to Rome to ride out the crisis. Three years later the Romans were able to counterattack and retook Jerusalem and their former territory in the eastern Mediterranean. They reinstalled Herod in his position. So now, even three decades later, when a group of

Parthians came to Judea looking for the new Jewish king, he was terrified.

At first that seems strange, doesn't it? To be scared by the people we sing about in "We Three Kings of Orient Are"? Well, the people in the song are not the same people who showed up at Herod's doorstep. First, though there were only three gifts, nothing in the Bible suggests there were only three people. There could have been just three or two hundred to three hundred. Second, these men most surely were not kings. Frankly, they were not even wise men per se, because when you think of "wise men," you think of older, professorial bookworms with long beards— maybe Gandalf the Grey or Albus Dumbledore. The Magi were primarily a warrior caste among the nobility. They were indeed educated—the Parthians were heirs of the great scientific and mathematical legacy of the Babylonians, including advances in astronomy. Most Magi were priests of Zoroaster, an eastern religion that has not entirely disappeared today.

Some, however, were true believers in the God that the Israelites worshiped. When the people of the southern kingdom were taken to Babylon in the sixth century B.C., captives like Daniel were promoted to the highest levels of the Babylonian and Persian governments. They passed down their faith for generations—thus there came to be some believers in the Parthian nobility. In addition to their wisdom, these Magi may have presented a physically imposing sight to Herod. Perhaps they were wearing military insignia. Parthian knights rode on warhorses and even wore scale armor, just like European knights of the Middle Ages.

That is why Herod was scared. I am sure it did not help that the first thing they said to him was, "Where's the one *born* king of the Jews?" Maybe he thought they were a commando team sent to assassinate him or the first wave of a Parthian military expedition that would drive him out of his kingdom and put this unknown baby in his place. He knew that he himself was a non-Jewish usurper with no legitimate right to the Judean "crown." Now comes talk of a baby who had been *born* to rule. Herod immediately went into self-preservation mode, and he crafted a lie. His plan was to get information about this challenger whom he perceived was going to try to take away the power that he had spent 40 years trying to keep. He was not going to worship this baby. He wanted to kill him.

They went on their way, and the star they had seen in the east went ahead of them until

it stopped over the place where the child was.
When they saw the star, they were overjoyed.
On coming to the house, they saw the child with
his mother Mary, and they bowed down and
worshiped him. Then they opened their trea-
sures and presented him with gifts of gold and
of incense and of myrrh. (Matthew 2:9-11)

By the time the Magi arrived, Mary and Joseph were not in a stable anymore. Joseph, the dear stepfather, had gotten his wife and new baby out of the barn and found a nearby house. Perhaps Mary explained to him that she wasn't quite ready to walk or ride a donkey 80 miles home right away. God's miracle star stopped over their Bethlehem rental home, which is where the Magi found the family and brought their baby gifts. Gold, incense, and myrrh are not typical baby gifts these days. (I bet Mary would have appreciated some disposable diapers.) Yet, these were the perfect gifts for that time.

Gold is always the metal of kings, isn't it? The Magi knew that this child was the King. I also think the gold turned out to be a practical gift. Joseph and Mary, who were not in their hometown near his carpentry shop, would need money to live off of for weeks until they could return to Nazareth. In God's kind advance provision, that gold was undoubtedly helpful for their living expenses during their exile in Egypt. The Magi also gave incense, a fragrant gum that could be collected off trees, and myrrh, another fragrant and expensive aromatic tree resin. At a time when most people did not bathe regularly, myrrh and incense were essential to help the house smell better. It could also be sold to help the little family's emergency living expenses.

It amazes me that these Gentile Magi left the safety of Parthia, went behind enemy lines, carried a fortune that could be ripped off or attacked, and risked the danger that Roman troops might slaughter them because they viewed the Magi's visit as an act of war. Yet they took all these risks, didn't they? Somehow God got the message to them about the identity of that baby, and they seized an opportunity to be with him in person—and to give him the welcome he deserved. They made this dangerous journey and gave their treasures because they recognized that the Messiah had come, their Messiah. Even though he was born like a beggar in a barn with a feed box for a crib, God had come in person to save his people. They came to worship their *Savior*.

They came to admire his great power, to acknowledge their smallness in front of his greatness, to kneel down and show their obedience to the One who could command them, but more than that, to love back the One who loved them enough to become incarnate. Messiah came to walk our walk, live under the laws of God and men, and carry them all out in our place. He became one of us to walk in the dust of our world, coming down here to this broken, sick, dysfunctional world and experiencing the fullness of human life in every way, to be hurt by our hurts, to wrestle with Satan as you and I have failed in doing so often, and to win that battle of wills. The Magi came a great and dangerous distance to say "Wow!" and "Thank you!" and "We love you, and we don't care what the risk or cost is. We want to have a chance to worship you perhaps before we die." They gave him their hearts, and they showed it with their lives and with their treasures, giving him gifts worthy of a king.

The Messiah's significance and value to you is no less than what it was to those Magi. They were Gentiles too, just like most of us. They were not part of the

Jewish race; neither are most of Messiah's worshipers today. They recognized who he was. They didn't come to do treaties or bargain with him. They came to *worship* their God. They perceived his identity and made him the focal point of what they did. At great personal risk and at great personal expense, they traveled a long, long way under dangerous circumstances to give their King gifts fit for a king. This is your mission too. Give yourself to your Savior. Give him the attention he deserves, the worship he deserves, and the gifts that he deserves, appropriate for the King of kings. He not only is your rescuer from damnation; he is also the Lord, who rules over all and protects you and has invited you to live with him in his eternal home.

Still, how do you do this? You can't physically travel to Jesus, because there is no Christmas star in the sky over a house anymore. Plus, the last time I checked, you cannot find incense or myrrh on any baby registry at your local megastore. So how can we be as generous and prepared as the Magi? To get ready for Jesus, to give him the royal welcome he deserves, let's go into the desert for an encounter with his prophetic cousin John.

In those days John the Baptist came, preaching in the Desert of Judea and saying, "Repent, for the kingdom of heaven is near." This is he who was spoken of through the prophet Isaiah:

"A voice of one calling in the desert, 'Prepare the way for the Lord, make straight paths for him.'" (Matthew 3:1-3)

There has never been anyone like John the Baptizer. What a location! Who but God would find the bleak wilderness of the lower Jordan valley a great place to connect with people? Here was somebody in an unusual place with an unusual message to shake people out of their comfort zones. His message began with the challenge, "Repent." The English language does not really do this concept justice. To us, *repent* sounds like a one-time deal, like a quick "I'm sorry." In the Greek language, it literally means to change your mind. John was really telling the people to "be repenting," i.e., to have an ongoing repentant attitude.

Be repenting. That is step one in getting ready for the Messiah. Each of us by nature has got his or her mind pointed in the wrong direction. John is telling you to reverse course and change your mind. Why?

Because the kingdom of heaven is just as near to you as it was to the people who went out into the desert to see John. Your opportunity to be part of God's gracious kingdom is right here. Now is the time; do not miss it. To be in God's kingdom means that you have a living relationship with the King—that you believe in him and he lives in you.

Back in John's day, the people were not ready for Christmas. Their mind-set was, "I have to *do* whatever God says. If I *obey* the rules and the laws, I will be okay. If I mess up, I'll bring my sacrifices, and then I will be okay." In our day, we slip into these ways of thinking too, isn't it so? We lurch between despair and pride. You tell yourself, "I'm a mess; I have not kept the commandments. I'm hopeless," or worse, "Compared to my neighbor, I am doing great. I've kept many of the rules (well, the important ones anyway), so I must be okay." That is why we need to listen to what John had to say. We need to change our mind-set. A place in God's kingdom cannot be earned by our behavior.

Matthew quotes Isaiah—the same Isaiah who prophesied to Ahaz had also prophesied about John. He said, *"A voice of one calling: 'In the desert prepare the way for the Lord; make straight in the wilderness a highway for our God. Every valley shall be raised up, every mountain and hill made low; the rough ground shall become level, the rugged places a plain'"* (Isaiah 40:3,4).

Think of yourself as a road grader to get a highway ready before the paving crew can come through. You know they must get the road laid straight. This is what you and I need to do right now to prepare for the celebration of the birth of Christ. First, we must repent about the mountains of our pride. We do need help because we are *not* fine just the way we are. Get out the road grader and level it down in humbleness for your own sins. Also, repent about your ditches of despair. We can fall into depression and feelings of worthlessness. Let the Lord Jesus fill in those valleys and remind you how precious you are to him. With Jesus in your heart and life, grade down your pride, fill in your despair, and give Jesus a level path to enter.

John's clothes were made of camel's hair, and he had a leather belt around his waist. His food was locusts and wild honey. People went out to him from Jerusalem and all Judea and the whole region of the Jordan. Confessing their sins, they were baptized by him in the Jordan River. (Matthew 3:4-6)

John was like no spiritual leader you've ever seen. His camel's hair clothes weren't made of the smooth, elegant coat fabric of today. It was an actual camel hide salvaged from a dead camel. His leather belt wasn't by Gucci—it was a strip of animal skin that he probably cut and scraped himself. His food wasn't designer honey—it was survival food. He probably got 50 bee stings every time he dipped into a hive for a meal. It is shocking to me that people from everywhere came to him. Would *you* have walked out into the desert to listen to a strange-looking poor man with a hard message? Well, you just might have, just as they did, because John was speaking the *truth*. These people knew their insides were sick, but they had no clue what to do about it—*until John told them*. So they began as he instructed, by confessing their sin. Unless you see what is wrong in you and what Jesus came to do, the good news of the Savior in the manger will be nothing but another cutesy little mythological December story.

Confessing means you acknowledge that you are accountable to a power higher than yourself. Instead of creating your own comfier standards, you allow God's rule book to be applied to you. You listen to the bad news that comes crashing down on commandment breakers and realize with humility that you have not measured up to the holiness that the Maker of this world requires.

I don't know about you, but I am squirming a bit just writing this, so I imagine you are shifting in your chair while reading it. Nobody actually likes to hear this message from John because we all have a little Satan inside of us. There is a part of us that *wants* to sin, that *likes* to sin, and that does not want to admit God's sovereignty over our lives. Still, the people went out into the uncomfortable desert and found the relief they were looking for. It works the same way for us. As part of the process of repentance, it feels *good* to unload your sins on the baby in the manger, to kneel down like the Magi did and say, "I need you, Messiah. You have what I do not have and can never buy or earn or achieve for myself."

The second step of the people's repentance was that they were baptized. Baptism is an extraordinary gift from God. It is not simply a ritual, an outward demonstration of obedience to help us earn some favor with God. Baptism is a direct encounter with your Savior. John had been telling anyone who would listen (and even those who wouldn't), *"Look, the Lamb of God, who takes away the sin of the world!*—your sin and mine" (John 1:29). The very sin that makes us unfit for God's presence is removed, not by our actions, but by the wonderful work of Jesus Christ. God chose to be born of a virgin, to be with us, to have flesh and blood, so he could live a perfect and innocent life as our substitute. He was stepping in for you so that at the end of his life he had flesh and blood to be able to offer it and to die your death and my death as a sacrificial Lamb. In this way he purchased forgiveness for your sins, all of your sins, and gives it to you.

Now when you are baptized into Christ, you are connected to the one who gives you what you could not achieve for yourself. God promises that *"all of you who were baptized into Christ have clothed yourselves with Christ"* (Galatians 3:27). No matter what age you were when the Lord touched you with that wonderful washing, his Word brought about a miracle and connected you with your Savior. This is not something you do for God. It is something he does for you. You are simply an empty-handed beggar who says thank you for cleaning me up, for putting beautiful spiritual clothes on me to cover the evil within. Now God can deal with us as though we had never sinned. And if that were not generous enough, God also uses

Baptism to put the Holy Spirit inside of us, to create the faith we need and allow us to continue to grow in faith and deeds. John speaks to that too.

> *John said to the crowds coming out to be baptized by him, "You brood of vipers! Who warned you to flee from the coming wrath? Produce fruit in keeping with repentance. And do not begin to say to yourselves, 'We have Abraham as our father.' For I tell you that out of these stones God can raise up children for Abraham. The ax is already at the root of the trees, and every tree that does not produce good fruit will be cut down and thrown into the fire."* (Luke 3:7-9)

John did not mince words. As the people were coming out to the desert to hear what he had to say, I would think he might have softened the message to get people to like him. Instead, he told them they were all venomous snakes. Would you even finish this paragraph if I said you were like a nest of snakes? Frankly, I don't have the nerve to say it because I know I am a viper myself. But John had the courage to say it, not because he had no sin, but because it was the truth. He wanted people to repent, or else they would be in for a nasty surprise when the humble baby returned to earth as their glorious judge. So he told them to start producing fruit. "Fruit" here is a figure of speech, meaning that you need to produce evidence that there is faith within you, so that God and other people can see that you are a Christian. In other words, now that you are wearing Jesus' robes of holiness, show them off. Not, however, in order to be saved, but because you are saved; it is simply the inevitable result of the Spirit living inside of you.

That idea used to confuse me until I lived in a house that had a great big pear tree in the backyard. That tree would bear its little pear heart out every year, producing more than I could eat or give away. Now—that tree did not produce pears so it could become a pear tree, but because it already was one. In the same way, God is intensely interested in the words you say, in the actions you do, in the value system you choose. Not as a reason for him to start liking you, but because you already are his. He has already given you the ability to repent, to confess your sins, to trust in the full forgiveness you have. He unchained you from the dead weight of your past and has given you his Holy Spirit to empower the new life. That explains why the Bible still talks about how urgently important it is for you to think and do and say things that are right, because that is evidence of a living faith within you.

Now, some of the people who went out to the desert were thinking that simply because they were Jewish—Abraham's children—they would be saved. Well, John was pretty clear that simply being Jewish wasn't enough. We are not saved by race, but by grace, through faith. Living faith always produces living fruit. Dead trees are cut down to make room for fruit-producing trees. Today John would not talk about axes. He would say that the chainsaws are revved up and at your ankles. God is bringing a day of accountability, and if it helps you to think of it in terms of a tree, ask yourself, "What kind of tree am I? Am I all leaves? Am I just wild growth? Or are there pears on my tree? Is there fruit in my life? Am I showing Christianity or am I dead?" Wow!

It is easy to think that because we are forgiven by Jesus, we can coast our way to the finish line. Not so. John's desert challenge is a wake-up call. Jesus saved you for a variety of reasons. One of the main ones is so that you can become *useful* to him, to transform you so you are able to serve the Lord, to serve other people, and to make his name look good to all the people who are still groping around looking for a God who is real. That is why a critically important part of being continually repentant, of making Jesus' path straight, of giving Jesus the welcome he deserves, is to let the good things he has planted within you produce fruit. It makes your faith visible.

"What should we do then?" the crowd asked.

John answered, "The man with two tunics should share with him who has none, and the one who has food should do the same."

Tax collectors also came to be baptized. "Teacher," they asked, "what should we do?"

"Don't collect any more than you are required to," he told them.

Then some soldiers asked him, "And what should we do?"

He replied, "Don't extort money and don't accuse people falsely—be content with your pay."
(Luke 3:10-14)

John's hearers were having trouble applying his teachings. What needed to be changed? They said what you would say: "Give us some examples." So he did. He told them to share, to quit stealing, to stop abusing people, to tell the truth. John wasn't scolding, nagging, or whining. He was not trying to scare them; he was not limiting Christian growth into just a few legal categories. They just needed some ideas, some illustrations of faith at work.

Frankly, I do too. Sometimes I cannot tell what trash in my life needs to be taken out because I am so full of self-deception. That is why it is good to ask those around you how you can lower your mountains and fill in your ditches—because sometimes other people can see the dysfunctions in your life a lot faster than you can. Don't believe me? If you truly aren't sure what needs to change in your life so that the Lord Jesus goes from being a bit player in your life to having the starring role, ask somebody close to you. I bet you get an answer within five seconds.

Now, maybe you know what you need to work on. Maybe you know already what sins in your life are keeping Jesus from being front and center. But if you, like the people in the wilderness, want an outsider's perspective, may I be so bold as to offer some ideas?

Maybe you have a violent mouth and words pour out that you would love to suck back in. Maybe your ability to manage anger could use an overhaul. Are you living together as husband and wife without being married? Don't do it. Are you fun to work with in the office, or do you bring so much personal baggage that negativity spills all around you? Maybe your children feel only pressure and disapproval from you, but what they are starving for is to know that you love them and accept them unconditionally.

Kids, when you give your parents abuse and guff, you are fighting against the very captains of the family boat that God has sent to bless you. Now would be a great time to take out the trash of your sassy mouth and replace your disrespect with something that would make Jesus feel more at home. Or maybe your life looks like it has been touched by King Midas—maybe everything is golden for you right now—and you begin to take credit for it. Give the glory to God where it belongs. Possibly you look at others around you and feel superior; you can see their weaknesses so quickly and easily. Bulldoze down that mountain of pride. You are morally no better than anybody else. Without the mercy of the Messiah, you too would be terrified on judgment day.

Before I wrap up this chapter, there is a mighty concept I need to make sure we are clear on. So I am going to say it again, because I will have failed miserably if you misunderstand me. It is this: *You do not have to change to get God to like you.* God accepts you as you are. He accepts you, warts and all. He accepts you with flaws. He accepts you, brokenness and all. He accepts you no matter what miserable state he finds you in and pronounces his love and forgiveness to you unconditionally. At the same time, the fact that he accepts you as you are *does not mean he settles for who you are.* You are a work in progress—emphasis on *work* and emphasis on *progress.* So when you produce fruit in keeping with repentance, do not do it in order to get God to like you, but *because* God already likes you. Not *in order* to be forgiven, but *because* you already are forgiven. Not *in order* to become a child of God, but *because* you already are one. Your identity has been changed. In Christ you are somebody else now; the Bible calls you a new creation.

This is how you give Jesus a happy birthday. You do not have to make him a cake, and you probably can't afford over two thousand candles. Instead, view the Magi as your personal heroes and examples and let the Baptist's blunt message guide you.

- First, repent. Recognize that your own self-generated holiness is completely inadequate to gain God's favor. Humble yourself and confess your need.
- Second, believe the Bible's message that the Father's unconditional love and the Son's pure self-sacrifice have paid all your debts and declared you to be precious and valuable.
- Third, praise God that his Word and his washing have created faith in your heart. Believe everything the Bible tells you about your Messiah.
- Fourth, treat Jesus like the King he is. Honor him with your words and deeds. Give him your equivalent of gold, incense, and myrrh. Let nothing stop you from committing your life to him. Treat your relationship with him as your most valuable possession.

Happy birthday to you. Happy birthday to you. Happy birthday, dear Jesus. Happy birthday to you!

Chapter 3

Where Will He Come From?

O little town of Bethlehem, how still we see thee lie!
Above thy deep and dreamless sleep
the silent stars go by.
Yet in thy dark streets shineth the everlasting light.
The hopes and fears of all the years
are met in thee tonight.

This chapter could be extremely short, couldn't it? One of the top ten Christmas hymns of all time gives away the answer to the question, Where will he come from? Still, I want to explore the little town of Bethlehem with you because of the amazing things God did in that humble but famous place. It really is true that "the hopes and fears of all the years"—of all of human history, in fact—came together there.

Galatians 4:4 tells us, *"When the time had fully come, God sent his Son,"* sent him to carry out the plan he once shared with Ahaz. It was time for Immanuel to start his journey to keep you and me from everlasting misery.

From Mary and Joseph's point of view (that is, if they were not thinking too deeply about these things), the birth *in Bethlehem* sure must have seemed like an accident. *They lived up north in Nazareth!* My guess is that Mary thought she still had some time before the baby would arrive. Maybe Mary's obstetrician or midwife got the due date wrong; no woman I know would intentionally walk or ride a donkey 80 miles when she was nine months pregnant. If she had known that she was due any day and they had still decided to risk the travel anyway, I think they would have made arrangements for a more comfortable place to stay each night.

In reality, when her contractions began in earnest, they were trapped in the crummiest, ugliest lodging you could imagine: a stable, barely one step up from camping in the open air. It was dark—the stable owners weren't going to waste expensive oil for all-night lamps in a cattle pen. Once Mary's labor began, I would guess that the animals couldn't sleep anymore, so the cows, donkeys, and sheep would have been making their unique noises and doing what animals do.

Add to that the nervous terror Joseph must have felt while watching his wife give birth. I can almost hear his audible prayers of "Help me, Lord!" while Mary moaned and sighed in her travails. It was a blessed relief once it was all over, as is usually the case with all births, but getting through it must have been the most horrible ordeal of their young lives.

From God's point of view, however, Mary and Joseph were exactly where they needed to be. Bethlehem as birthplace was no accident. For thousands of years, God had been planning his rescue mission and had shared his plans bit by bit. What the believers did not know was *when* it would happen. I am confident the shepherds in the fields nearby were not expecting the sky to light up that night with angels telling them that the Messiah had finally come. Still, once they learned that God had kept his promise, they ran to the manger, saw the baby, and then told everybody they met what they had seen.

It was the day everyone was waiting for. They all knew the coming Savior was going to arrive in Bethlehem; the Scriptures said so. When the Magi came from the East, they asked King Herod, "We're looking for the king that's to be born. Where would that be?" When Herod asked his team of religious advisors, they knew the answer right away—Bethlehem. How did they know the very spot on the face of the earth where those promises of the Lord for many centuries were going to come true? Because they paid attention to what the prophet Micah said.

This beautiful nugget of a promise, identifying the very spot that Immanuel would be born seven and a half centuries before it happened, is embedded in a larger setting. God allowed Micah to see the future— some of it so good the people could barely fathom it, some so miserable it was nightmarish. The setting at the time in which God shared another part of his plan makes the good news even more meaningful.

The prophet Micah had both the advantage and misery of living sometime around 750 to 730 B.C. In his lifetime, he witnessed the disintegration of the northern kingdom of Israel, which was attacked and destroyed by the Assyrians. Many of the people were deported. The southern kingdom of Judah and its capital of Jerusalem survived a while longer, but at Micah's time it was nothing but a rump of its former wealth and power during the days of David and Solomon.

Remember the story of how Isaiah prophesied to Ahaz that King Pekah would die and the northern kingdom would be crushed? Micah and his contemporaries saw that prophecy come true, but he did not want his fellow people of Judah and Jerusalem to laugh at the plight of their neighbors to the north. In fact, Judah did not escape assault by the Assyrians through military might; the Assyrians left Judah alone for the time being because they were paid off. Judah's reprieve was only temporary. Their own time was coming, and Micah had some sobering words for them, though their coming tormentors would not be the Assyrians.

Writhe in agony, O Daughter of Zion, like a woman in labor, for now you must leave the city to camp in the open field. You will go to Babylon; there you will be rescued. There the LORD will redeem you out of the hand of your enemies.

But now many nations are gathered against you. They say, "Let her be defiled, let our eyes gloat over Zion!" But they do not know the thoughts of the LORD; they do not understand his plan, he who gathers them like sheaves to the threshing floor. (Micah 4:10-12)

Micah uses a deeply significant nickname for Jerusalem—he calls her "Zion." The original meaning of this term referred to the slender but steep north/south ridge on which the original city was built. By extension, *Zion* became a metaphor for all of Jerusalem and her inhabitants. Micah's message to them is essentially this: "You dodged the sword this time, Jerusalem, but don't you laugh. Your time is coming, and it will be miserable." Ask any mother to share her birthing stories, and she will openly and elaborately tell you about the temporary agony she endured. That writhing in agony is Micah's metaphor for how bad it would be during the final assault by a new menace: Babylon.

At the time Micah wrote, Babylon was merely one of the administrative regions of the gigantic Assyrian Empire. Perhaps his original hearers blew off the significance of the message because they didn't see Babylon as a threat. What a threat it was! In 150 years the Babylonians would burn Jerusalem to the ground. Compounding the humiliation, all the nations around them would gloat and enjoy their suffering, like when a gang gets one of its enemies in a back alley and gives him a beating. The thugs stand around during the beat down and yell, "Give it to him. Yeah, hit him again."

Those surrounding nations, who may have been gloating at Judah's misfortune, never knew that behind everything was God and his plans. The Bible helps us understand that God uses governments as he sees fit for his holy agenda. From the moment he set them apart, God had lavished attention on his people Israel. He was not primarily interested in making them into a world military superpower like the Romans, nor did he want them to be so wealthy that they would grow arrogant and corrupt. Instead, he wanted a nation of *believers*, people who would treasure his words, guard them, transmit them to their children, learn them, live them, and share them with the world. This is why Israel proper was not by a sprawling landmass like Russia, but rather a sliver of land on the main line of communication in the ancient world, a high-traffic corridor where three continents joined together. But when God's people generally lost interest in him, they necessitated a tough-love approach. So, though he would ultimately rescue his people, God planned to use other countries to take away Israel's military power, then their wealth, and soon their political independence as well.

Marshal your troops, O city of troops, for a siege is laid against us. They will strike Israel's ruler on the cheek with a rod. (Micah 5:1)

Micah now calls Jerusalem by another nickname—"O city of troops"—and tells them to prepare for war. For years the people of Jerusalem thought they were invulnerable, but he tells them, "You trust in your heavy walls to protect you. You trust in the trenches you're digging. You trust in your internal water supply that you think nobody can get. You trust in your military plans and preparedness. You think you're bulletproof (okay, swordproof). Well, guess what? Get ready because another country is coming to starve you out."

Not only would the country fall apart, but it would lose its leaders; the dynasty of the kings of Judah would come to an end. Back then, as they received guests in their throne rooms, kings carried a golden mace, a symbolic representation of a war club used to strike and crush an opponent's skull. When a ruler was able to smite his opponent in the face with a rod, that meant that the last line of defense was gone.

Game over. Checkmate. That imagery was so widely known and understood that Assyrian and Egyptian royal military art, both painting and stone carving, would often depict a triumphant king personally clubbing his defeated foe.

That happened to Judah, both figuratively and literally. One Jewish king had a fishhook put in his nose deliberately to humiliate him as he was taken off to captivity. Another, Zedekiah, was forced, in chains, to watch his children killed before his eyes. Then his eyes were gouged out so his last visual memories would be of the slaughter of his children.

I don't know about you, but right about now I am not getting any cozy, cuddly Christmas feelings. Why in the world, in the passages leading up to God's sweet promise to little Bethlehem, would he put this dreadful story in his Word for us? My first suggestion is because he is cautioning you never to get careless with God's words. Never get so full of yourself that you believe you do not need God anymore. By nature we all stand guilty in God's court. Every one of us, in many ways, has joined Satan's conspiracy to declare war against God. This is a wake-up call to everybody, to accept these hard words and get on our knees in repentance and say, "Lord, if we got what we had coming, there would be people coming to smash *us* in the cheek with an iron stick as well."

A second reason might be that God wants us to see that not all pain is bad. Not all disasters are disasters. If our hardships, either those he sent or those we inflict on ourselves, bring us to repentance and result in a renewed faith and hope in God, God's agenda is successful. He works it both ways. He is faithful and rock-steady in his purpose to draw people into an eternal relationship with him.

> *"But you, Bethlehem Ephrathah, though you are small among the clans of Judah, out of you will come for me one who will be ruler over Israel, whose origins are from of old, from ancient times."* (Micah 5:2)

Here comes the good news (finally!). Big, mighty Jerusalem, the city of troops, the royal capital, would fall. But dinky little Bethlehem—God chose you! You have an enormous role in God's rescue plans for the human race, and you are about to get even more special. Most people already had a soft spot for Bethlehem, which in Hebrew means "house of bread." Not only was it a good place for growing grain and also a great place for pasturing livestock, it also was the site of a slew of significant events in the history of the people of Israel.

To start, Abraham had lived just a little to the south of Bethlehem. Then, Jacob's second wife, Rachel, died while giving birth to Benjamin, and she was buried there. Her tomb became a national holy place. After the Israelites wandered in the desert for 40 years, Caleb, one of two spies who reported they could indeed take the land of Canaan as God had promised, was given a significant tract of land to farm in that vicinity. He named its town "Ephrah," or "Ephrath," after his second wife (this is why it is called "Bethlehem Ephrathah" in Micah chapter 5).

Not long after that, when Israel did take over Canaan, a man named Salmon moved there. You might have never heard of him, but he was the prince and executive leader of the entire tribe of Judah. Also—he had a famous wife, a former prostitute named Rahab, who played a prominent role in helping the Israelites take over Jericho. Rahab and Salmon had a son named Boaz, who was a successful bachelor farmer. Boaz later in life took a wife named Ruth, another woman who was not from the line of God's people. Ruth and Boaz had a grandson named Jesse, and Jesse was the father of David, the second king of Israel. David grew up tending sheep on Bethlehem's hills. Even after David established his capital in the city of Jerusalem, he remained loyal to and loved his hometown. Fast-forward 28 generations and little Bethlehem would be in Bible news again.

When Caesar Augustus said it was time to count all the people in his kingdom, Joseph went *"to Bethlehem the town of David, because he belonged to the house and line of David"* (Luke 2:4). Today, when the United States takes a census, they either mail you a form or show up at your front door. Back in the day, the Romans required citizens to travel back to their ancestors' hometown. Because Joseph was David's descendant and claimed the tiny city of David as his ancestral home, he made plans for a short trip. He and Mary decided that Mary would come too.

Interesting, isn't it, how God set the entire Roman Empire in motion to get his chosen woman into the chosen town? Finally, seven and a half centuries after he first made the promise, God said the time was right for Bethlehem to be front and center on the world's stage. He brought Mary and Joseph from their home-town of Nazareth, about 80 miles as the crow flies, longer if you count the bends in the roads, to just the right place, at just the right time, just as he said he would. Here, in little Bethlehem, from the house of David, God raised up one last, great, eternal King. As sweet as his promise to Bethlehem was, the promise of what this King would be like was even sweeter to the people of Israel, who had lived through a long line of very bad kings. Those kings far too often used their power only to enrich themselves and to hurt others, but this King, your King, the immortal King Jesus Christ, came to *help* you.

> *Therefore Israel will be abandoned until the time when she who is in labor gives birth and the rest of his brothers return to join the Israelites.*

> *He will stand and shepherd his flock in the strength of the LORD, in the majesty of the name of the LORD his God. And they will live securely, for then his greatness will reach to the ends of the earth. And he will be their peace.*
> (Micah 5:3-5)

God was more interested in the people than in the power. He gave no permanent divine guarantees to Israel's wealth, political organization, or armies, which is why Israel would be dismantled and look abandoned until Mary gave birth. At that time, and not before, he would give them their King back. But it wouldn't be the earthly kingdom they expected. Everything would change. The new kingdom would look very, very different. Why? Because it includes you! When Micah says that *"the rest of his brothers return to join the Israelites,"* he is talking about the lost Gentile brothers and sisters—you and me. When Jesus came, he opened up the gates, opened up his arms, and the great influx of Gentiles joined the family of God.

Now, for both Jews and Gentiles, for eyewitnesses of Jerusalem's fall, for subjects of the Roman Empire, and for 21st-century moderns, Micah pours out hope and good news. He tells you just *how* Bethlehem's King will rule. When he wrote *"he will stand and shepherd them,"* Micah did not need to elaborate, because the people of Bethlehem were familiar with a shepherd's résumé. For those of us who do not live in sheep territory (and I am guessing that's a fair number), let's briefly review a shepherd's job description. First, shepherds guide their sheep. Sheep back then, living in an arid climate, did not have the benefit of maps or GPS. If it weren't for the shepherd, they would *never* have gotten to the next pasture or found water. They would die in the heat. Believers are the Lord's sheep; alas, we easily get lost too. Christ, your personal Shepherd, knows you cannot always see your way through this world, knows that your natural tendency is to put yourself in danger, and knows that you need his guidance.

Our planet, our culture, and our civilization have no moorings of right and wrong. It is our curse to live in an age of relativism, where societal and cultural leaders sincerely believe that there are no moral absolutes. We are taught that we descended from animals, and so we act like animals. We degenerate into materialism and violence, selfishness and greed. Jesus changes that. He promises to walk with you through your life and helps you make decisions about where you are going.

This does not mean he will fill the sky with a pillar of cloud and fire as in olden days to guide you or call you on your mobile device to tell you whether or not to take the job offer. He has given you his Word to help you understand where you are going and to get your value system set up right. He puts Christian people in your life to give you wise advice. He gives you a brain and reasoning and his Spirit to live within to guide that brain. He gives you the precious privilege of a direct throne hotline we call prayer. Isaiah promises believers, *"Whether you turn to the right or to the left, your ears will hear a voice behind you, saying, 'This is the way; walk in it'"* (Isaiah 30:21).

Another job of shepherds is to *feed* their sheep. When you pray the Lord's Prayer and ask our Savior-Shepherd, Jesus, to "give us today our daily bread," he joyfully answers that prayer and personally sees to all of your physical, emotional, and spiritual needs. He may not give you everything you *want*, but you will not lack what he thinks you *need*. In addition, God feeds your mind and spirit with his Word. In his amazing Supper that we call Communion, you actually receive the Shepherd's body and blood, the very price paid to forgive your sins. You become one with him and he with you. You cannot possibly mistake your Shepherd's intention to connect with you personally. Word and Sacrament build your faith, increase your spiritual stamina, and develop your personal gifts and talents for service to him and other people.

His third job as Shepherd is to *protect* you. Sheep are tasty, vulnerable animals—and so are you. Just as shepherds look out for natural predators, King Jesus knows you have a roaring lion seeking to devour you.

Jesus watches over you, puts his arms around you, and sends his angels to protect you so Satan cannot tear you to shreds. Every time you pray "lead me not into temptation, but deliver me from evil," you are asking your Shepherd, who is more powerful than Satan, to keep a force field around you. Jesus already went to war against the lion when he put his own body between you and your worst enemy. Because the Bethlehem King won, his sheep, you and I, *"will live securely, for then his greatness will reach to the ends of the earth. And he will be their peace."*

This Bethlehem King, who is looking out for his people, started life in a miserable way, laid in a donkey's feed box in a lowly town. He ended his life in an ugly way, nailed to a cross. Even the in-between years were not easy. He lived a perfect life to make up for your disobedience. He suffered a perfect death so your death will simply be a doorway through which you get real life. He defeated death by rising from the dead to guarantee that you will never have to experience hell's horrors.

Until that final day, though, it may seem as if you are still pretty sinful, suffering oppression and captivity just like the people of God at the time of Micah. Yet, right now, as a subject of the Bethlehem King, you have the forgiveness that rids you of guilt, panic, fear, and hopelessness. By giving you a royal pardon, the Lord Jesus tells you that you are worth something—worth dying for. Micah said, *"He will be your peace."* Do you believe that? Did it occur to you that this is your best Christmas gift ever? His love, his forgiveness, and his hope free you from your enemy's mastery and guilt. Right now, as we are waiting for the fullness of Christ's peace in heaven, let him give you a down payment. Though you may have chaos and various messes in your life right now, let Christmas peace live in your heart.

"Messiah is coming! Where will he come from?" The answer, "From Bethlehem," connects us to a rich and complex story of God's direct intervention in human history. It is a look at the past—to wonder at a God who would tell people 750 years ahead of time, in the midst of societal collapse, exactly where he would enter our world. It is a look at the present—how, even when we bring misery on ourselves by our selfishness, God calls us back and offers hope. And it is a look at the future—how the Shepherd-King born in Bethlehem will be our eternal peace.

O holy Child of Bethlehem, descend to us, we pray;

Cast out our sin and enter in; be born in us today.

We hear the Christmas angels the

great glad tidings tell;

Oh, come to us, abide with us, our Lord Immanuel!

Chapter 4

What Did He Come to Do?

One of my jobs at home is what I call "perimeter security." Before I go to bed, I check the doors to make sure they are all locked. Because I am the one who pays the utility bill in our home, I am also the official light-switcher-off-er, going around turning off the many lights that my tribe has left burning in the house. There is one problem with being the official light-switcher-off-er. It is a dangerous job at night. The last stretch to the bedroom is the riskiest part. Inevitably, once or twice a month, I am walking through the darkened upstairs hallway and can't see that a dear family member has left something on the floor. Whack! I hit my shin or stub my toe and try not to wake up the household as I hop around grunting in agony.

It is easy enough to blame other people for my run-ins in the dark. The problem is that I can run into stuff even in broad daylight. Maybe you have the same problem. You forget the coffee table has been moved, so you take too sharp a corner and whack it with your shin. Or maybe you are not paying attention and bonk into a doorframe with your head or bruise your hip on a counter edge. We all suffer bruises and wounds like that. However, imagine if you are truly blind. I don't know this for sure, but I would guess if you look at the shins of most people who have complete vision loss, you would see a lot of scars and bruises from all the things they have bumped into as they are navigating through life.

The prophet Isaiah talks about darkness and blindness as a metaphor for people who do not know God and who cannot explain the world they live in. They don't know, for instance, where we came from. Back when Isaiah was writing, the people who lived in Canaan were absolutely convinced that the Lord of the universe was a god named Baal. They believed that Baal and Asherah—who was both his wife and sister in their mythology—oversaw the human race and were the powers behind why things happened. Today, we would look at their religions and dismiss them as mere idolatries. If you lived in Babylon, you would have believed that Marduk and Ishtar were the god and goddess of the world and made things happen. We smugly look back at that today and say, "Nobody believes in that stuff; that's ridiculous."

But if the Babylonians and Canaanites could look at our world today, they would see the same thing— man-made religious systems populated by man-made gods, and they would sneer too. They would also see people who are convinced that there is no God at all, people who propose explanations for the development of the universe that deny any divine influence. What passes for great and deep wisdom today says that everything happens by random chance, that somehow a spontaneously big explosion turned inorganic matter into plants and soil and cells. Spontaneously, i.e., without design, cells turned into animals, and animals turned into people.

Without God, the true designer of the world, to reveal how things came to be, we grope around in darkness and have no idea about the meaning of the human race. The great British philosopher Bertrand Russell said, "When I die, I shall rot." In other words, there's absolutely no divine significance or meaning to my life, and after my descendants forget about me, other than some scraps of paper or maybe some electronic records, I shall cease to exist. Without revelation, without explanation from the designer, we would indeed have no idea what awaits us. Well, we may think we do or we make up explanations to help gloss over our fears, but those self-made ideas do not give the truth. By nature we are all in the dark, compelled to make up our own religious stories. One of the great gifts that our Bethlehem birthday boy came to bring is to switch on the lights for people, then and now, who are blind and stumbling around in darkness.

In this little book you have read a number of Old Testament prophesies so far. For many centuries the Israelites were waiting, waiting, waiting for the Messiah, waiting for the virgin to conceive, waiting for Immanuel ("God with us"), waiting for Bethlehem. Both Isaiah and Micah, who lived around the same time, witnessed the disintegration of the northern kingdom. Both of them foretold the destruction and collapse of the southern kingdom of Judah, which happened 150 years later. But God allowed them to see it so clearly that it was as if it had happened already. From his vantage point, because he can move freely through time, it already *has* happened. God has already been in our future; in fact, he is there now.

As a gift to us, he allowed Isaiah to see a slideshow of what was coming. Some of the slides (seven centuries in advance) tell us what our Messiah came to do.

> *Nevertheless, there will be no more gloom for those who were in distress. In the past he humbled the land of Zebulun and the land of Naphtali, but in the future he will honor Galilee of the Gentiles, by the way of the sea, along the Jordan.* (Isaiah 9:1)

This is finally a happy beginning to a prophecy. I am sure you have noticed so far that most of the chapters in this book began with some bad news from the prophets. Well, I have nothing on Isaiah who, quite frankly, loaded most of chapters 1-39 in his book with dreadful warnings and prophesies. Solid reasons exist for why the first half of Isaiah's book in the Bible is often called the "Book of Desolation." It was his task to pass along bad news for Israel, Judah, and the nations around them, all because of the massive tidal wave of human sin and their acts of rebellion against God. In the midst of that hard message are some beautiful nuggets of hope. Here is one of them: *"There will be no more gloom."* The oppressive dread and guilt that hung over the people then would be taken away. For those who are in distress now, the dank fog will lift.

First, Isaiah looks at a particular piece of geography. Zebulun and Naphtali, farm country, were Israel's tribal regions way up in the north, what people today might call the backwoods. Another reason people in cosmopolitan Jerusalem looked down on the tribal lands of Zebulun and Naphtali was they worried the northern area was getting way too Gentile. The area is also called "Galilee of the Gentiles," because the frontier between the Jewish Galileans and the Gentiles of Lebanon and Syria was a little porous—a lot of Greek-speaking people now lived together with the Jews in the northeast. It was the sad destiny of the northern tribes always to get hammered first. They were on the Assyrians' principal invasion path and were the first to lose their towns to invasion and captivity.

After centuries of scorn and invasion fears, Isaiah says God would *honor* that region when Jesus came. The tribal region of Zebulun was where Nazareth was located. The Savior of the world spent more time on earth in his hometown of Nazareth than anywhere else. Naphtali was the curved area around the Sea of Galilee, where Jesus spent two-thirds of his three-year ministry living and working in those small cities.

By sending the Savior to live and work there while on earth, God brought honor to these two previously "low self-esteem" tribes.

> *The people walking in darkness have seen a great light; on those living in the land of the shadow of death a light has dawned. You have enlarged the nation and increased their joy; they rejoice before you as people rejoice at the harvest, as men rejoice when dividing the plunder. For as in the day of Midian's defeat, you have shattered the yoke that burdens them, the bar across their shoulders, the rod of their oppressor. Every warrior's boot used in battle and every garment rolled in blood will be destined for burning, will be fuel for the fire. For to us a child is born, to us a son is given, and the government will be on his shoulders. (Isaiah 9:2-6)*

Jesus, announced in the sky by a star so bright that Magi from thousands of miles away could see it, is himself a bright star. In Malachi 4:2 the prophet calls Jesus *"the sun of righteousness,"* with healing in the rays that emanate from his face and in the words that come out of his mouth. He brings light, clarity, and truth to people who struggle and wallow in Satan's darkness and lies.

His light also shines on those who are pursued by death. And aren't we all? Who talks about death without fear, knowing it stalks you and the people you love? You still cry at the funeral of your great-grandma, even though she reached the ripe old age of 95. Each parent's greatest fear is that his or her child may be claimed. All of us want to go to heaven, but the dying part terrifies us. The gloomy cloud hovers around us, because we know death will, hopefully later rather than sooner, eventually get us all. What compounds our fear of the darkness is the guilt we feel because we know we deserve it. Deep down we know that death is a punishment, not something sweet and natural. Unless relieved by Jesus Christ, there is no other good, healthy way to get rid of the guilt.

You are intimately acquainted with rebellion. Though you are not perhaps a Baal or Buddha wor-shiper, you have found other idols to worship. Though you were not in the Garden of Eden with that fruit and the serpent, in various ways you have reenacted Adam and Eve's sin, haven't you? You have rebelled against God. Not only have you done it, but you also have even *liked* it. You know the adrenaline rush of losing your temper or the sick thrill of taking what does not belong to you. You know the lure of the freedom of doing what you want, of expressing your will and pushing God so far in the back you can hardly even hear his voice. You know the excitement of tying up your conscience, putting a gag in its mouth, shoving it in a closet, and closing the door so you cannot hear the little voice that says, "No!" That is part of the darkness inside. You know it and have felt it.

Even though the Israelites had piled up mountains of sin and unworthiness, God shared some more gracious good news. He said he was going to enlarge the nation and increase their joy. Seriously! At the time Isaiah wrote, the nation was not enlarging, it was collapsing. In fact, Israel was disintegrating before his very eyes. But he foresaw that God was not done with foolish little Israel, in spite of all its sins. God was going to stick with it and guarantee that the nation would accomplish its purpose. This is comforting for you because God is committed to sticking with you too. Even if your life right now does not seem all that happy, God will increase *your* joy. He can see your future, and he is actively involved in making it better, whether that happens here in this life or by taking you to be with him in heaven. The coming of the Messiah gives people walking in darkness, people like you, a reason to rejoice.

In the next part of this Scripture, Isaiah uses examples of the relief people will feel, using terminology they would understand. Just as we may have needed a little explaining about shepherd culture in the previous chapter, city folks may need some more explanation about Isaiah's agricultural references.

"As people rejoice at the harvest . . ." To be honest, I am a city guy and have no idea how I would make my living off the land. But a friend of mine does, and he often shares with me stories of his farm. One year, during the time when they planted, there was drought when they really needed rain to establish the crops. Then, at harvest, when they wanted it nice and dry, the rains came and came and came and they could not get into the fields. Farmers that year were running their combines in late November. When they finally got that last load in just before the snow fell, their relief was intense. Harvesters are exuberant when their source of income is safely in the barn.

". . . as men rejoice when dividing the plunder." At the end of a battle if you are still alive, you want to shout, "Woo-hoo! It's over! I made it!" Back in the day, after you won the fierce hand-to-hand combat,

you had the right to strip your dead enemies of their armor, weapons, and whatever else they were carrying. Then you went to their camp to rest up, eat all their food, and take their gold and jewels. Imagine the celebrating that went with plundering your mortal enemy's camp!

"You have shattered the yoke that burdens them, the bar across their shoulders, the rod of their oppressor." Unfortunately, slavery and imprisonment were a big part of Israelite life. First they were slaves in Egypt, then captives to the Assyrians, and finally imprisoned and used as forced labor for the Babylonian government. But God was going to draw the line. Never again would evil forces oppress and torment his people.

"Every warrior's boot used in battle and every garment rolled in blood will be destined for burning." This is another piece of God's good news in this section. The Israelites were battle-weary people. After all the wars they fought, their boots were worn and their clothes were covered in blood—theirs and the enemy's. But now that is over. There will be no more bloody uniforms when Messiah comes. They will not need weapons of war. In fact, everything associated with the battles would be burned.

Normally babies do not affect world events, but this one, this birth, changes everything. These four pieces of good news are going to come true, all because of *this* baby, *this* Son. When Messiah comes he is going to be in charge of everything. Now, if you need someone to save the universe, it would probably never occur to you to send a baby. Yet that is exactly what you needed. You needed Jesus Christ to be born for you and relive your life for you so you could get *his* credit report and he could take *yours*. By doing that, he carried everything—the government, the believers, the church, everything in the universe, on his shoulders. Now maybe you are thinking of the Greek god Atlas. The people of Greece envisioned him carrying the whole world on his shoulders. Atlas' story is a myth. Jesus Christ's is not. He actually does carry the world, and he rules over it and cares for it. Nothing is too heavy for him, including your cares.

And he will be called Wonderful Counselor, Mighty God, Everlasting Father, Prince of Peace. (Isaiah 9:6)

You might have been expecting Isaiah to switch back to bad news, but he is on a good-news roll from

God and just keeps pouring out the love and hope. Now he shares four astounding names for our Bethlehem baby. These names also help tell you what he came to do for you and for all people.

First, Jesus is our *Wonderful Counselor.* He is the one who explains where you came from, that you are a beautiful design, an engineering miracle of God. You did not evolve out of a swamp; you were designed to be amazing, exactly the way you are. God also designed the beauty and joy of the people around you. The Wonderful Counselor, like a guiding shepherd, also tells you why he made you that way, what your purpose is for living. He made you to be a miniature version of himself. You are a junior version of Christ, reflectors of his light in the world.

Your reason for being here is the same reason for Jesus' mission to be here, to bring hope and life to people who are gloomy and blindly stumbling. Because the Counselor has told you, you know where you are going and you can flip the light on for other people. Let them know that they too are beautifully designed, that because the Messiah came we have the gift of hope and peace now and the eternal privilege of being glorified and purified of every weakness. Immanuel ("God with us") came so that we will be princesses and princes of heaven, brothers and sisters, corulers with Christ in the heavenly mansions. That is your destiny. You know it is true because the Wonderful Counselor tells you all that in his Word.

Second, we hear that our Shepherd-King is *Mighty God.* The Israelites had plenty of experience with their mighty God. The stories of his power were handed down from generation to generation. Everyone knew that Father Abraham had a son when he was extremely old and that God spared him from sacrificing Isaac on an altar. They sang psalms that praised the ruler of the universe for holding back the waters of the Red Sea back when he led the captives out of Egypt. Their rock-solid God made the great walls of Jericho fall, while they simply walked around the city and cheered. Their hero, King David, was just a teenager when God used him and a smooth stone to kill Goliath. And it was well known that the prophet Elijah called on this mighty God to rain down fire from heaven on an altar soaked with water. Now, the same God who did all that is the same God who would fuse himself to a human body and become a one-man salvation team.

Third, Jesus is the *Everlasting Father* to his people. He has taken upon himself the obligations of father-hood toward you. He provides for you, as a shepherd provides for his sheep. Jesus gives you everything you need—maybe not everything you want, but everything you need. He protects you. All day he performs a constant perimeter security check. He sends his holy angels to limit the destructiveness of what the evil one is trying to do to your life. And instead of turning off the lights, he is the official light-switcher-on-er. He takes you by your hand and makes sure you never stumble in the dark again.

Isaiah shares a fourth name. Jesus is the *Prince of Peace.* Perhaps you have had terrifying guilt, thinking God is punishing you and you are getting what you deserve. Or maybe you dread facing God because you feel miserable and do not much like yourself. Though you may have given up on yourself, Jesus never gives up on you. He is the Peace of Prince, announcing that all is well with your God, not because of what you have done but because of what this Prince was coming to do. You are pardoned and forgiven by the shedding of the wonderful, holy blood of God himself. You are wearing Christ's robes of holiness through your faith and through your baptism.

No matter what has gone on in your past, though the pile of your sin smells like a garbage dump, Jesus' forgiveness is bigger than any mountain of sins you have been able to amass. You do not have to be afraid of your meeting with God. In fact, the Prince of Peace assures you that you look mighty good to your mighty God. Because of him there is peace on earth and good-will to those on whom his favor rests. What an almost unbelievable Christmas gift!

> *Of the increase of his government and peace there will be no end. He will reign on David's throne and over his kingdom, establishing and upholding it with justice and righteousness from that time on and forever. The zeal of the* Lord *Almighty will accomplish this.* (Isaiah 9:7)

Right when it seems the believers are doomed, Isaiah is allowed to peek at the future. What looks like collapsing on the outside is actually God's amazing, ultimate plan to explode the reign of King Messiah. An *increase* of government and peace? No end of it? The war-weary people of the northern kingdom and the southern kingdom of Israel would lose their lands, their armies, their possessions, and be taken off into captivity. Still, God's plan for them would be accomplished. David's line would not be permanently cut off, thanks to this child, this Son, this King.

For the faithful remnant of believers who had to live under a string of selfish, foolish, war-mongering rulers, the promise of this King's rule might have seemed too much to believe. He would be just? He would be righteous? I can almost picture them saying, "This sounds great, Isaiah, but pardon us for not wanting to get our hopes up too much." Yet that is exactly what God says will happen. All will be done right. All the curses and the punishment for our sins will be laid upon him. In God's divine justice, the believers will be given the righteousness—the rightness with God—they do not deserve. And this is how it is going to be from that time on until forever, all because God wants it to be that way. That is the grand finale of Isaiah's description of Messiah's work. God is zealous for you; he burns to do this for you because he knows how much you need it. He's crazy in love with you and spent centuries of effort to set up your divine rescue.

After reading all these portions, are you a little jealous of the Israelites? While his people were waiting for the Messiah to come, God talked to them through prophets, *directly*. They received specific guidance for specific situations. Now, I am not jealous of all the *bad* news they received, but—deep down inside—sometimes I wish we had those kinds of messengers today. People like Isaiah and Micah were stand-ins for Christ while God's people were waiting for that first Christmas. You know what? We are waiting for Christ too. While I wait, I have questions, and I am guessing you do too. Questions such as, why is God letting this happen to me? Or, how will my children turn out? Or, is there really a God who actually even cares about me? Or, what has this supposedly caring God done for me personally? When we don't perceive direct answers, it may be tempting to think that Immanuel has left the building and "God isn't with us" anymore.

But God says, "Hold on now. You do not need Isaiah or Micah to talk to you about me. You get something even better." In three sentences in the New Testament book of Hebrews, God lets us see even more of his extraordinary plan by telling us even more about who Jesus is and what he came to do.

In the past God spoke to our forefathers through
the prophets at many times and in various ways,
but in these last days he has spoken to us by

his Son, whom he appointed heir of all things, and through whom he made the universe.
(Hebrews 1:1,2)

Only God knew when the time would be right for him to send Jesus into the world. While the rest of the world was waiting for that, God sent messages to his prophets about things he wanted his people to know. He bridged the distance between his people and himself—distance that they brought on themselves—by making sure that the people knew what he was up to. He wanted them to know of his judgment and hatred for their sin, but know also about his love for them and acceptance of them as individuals. He wanted them to know his burning desire to have a permanent long-term relationship with them. But those were preliminary messengers only. Their work had no independent validity outside of the coming of Christ. It was he who anointed all their work and made it real. It was he whose coming completed and fulfilled and validated what they had said. In Christ it all made sense.

Just by coming and being born, Jesus was an immense, nonverbal message sent to the world. First of all, God came *in person* to bridge the gap between his holiness and our sin. Caught up in that little baby's body was the fullness of humanity, as human as you are, except for your sin. Jesus Christ shares every aspect of your humanity, every feature of life, even the birth experience. But he also carries the fullness of God himself. In fact, the very name of this miracle baby, Jesus, comes from the Hebrew word *Yeshua,* which means "the Lord saves." It says that he came to meet our greatest need, which was to be rescued. He was the last and greatest of all of the prophets, sent to earth to communicate a wonderful message of God's love. In person.

Another extraordinary claim in this passage is that God says he made the universe through Jesus. Remember where the gospel of John says, *"The Word became flesh and made his dwelling among us"* (John 1:14)? Words exist to communicate. *The* Word, i.e., a beautiful metaphor for Jesus Christ, came to earth in person to communicate God's primary message. The One who made us came to see, right up close, the people he had made and had come to rescue. He wants us to know, "I'm your Creator. I made you in my image to be like me. You're not pathetic and worthless; you're not small and unworthy of my concern. You're not a throwaway. You are not disposable. I'm not tired of you. You have value to me." He came in person to make sure you know that your existence is not the result of utter coincidence and mere chance. He made you intentionally, and he came in person to take you back into his family.

> *The Son is the radiance of God's glory and the exact representation of his being, sustaining all things by his powerful word. After he had provided purification for sins, he sat down at the right hand of the Majesty in heaven.*
> (Hebrews 1:3)

The glory of the Lord had left the people of Israel, which is why they were stumbling. When the temple in Jerusalem was destroyed by the Babylonians, as both Micah and Isaiah prophesied, the bright cloud of glory of God's presence stayed away until God said the time was right. Then, when Jesus Christ came to earth, the glory of God came flooding back. So when Christ came in person, he brought an incredible message to a confused, broken, and lost human race. God said, "I am here. Look at his face and see my glory." What comfort that brought to people who were terrified that the presence and glory of the Lord had been removed and would never come back. You know that terror too, don't you? Those terrible moments of fear when it seems God's throne is empty and the glory is gone. You look around and see there is nothing but us—and we are spinning out of control. Jesus came in person so you would know the glory of God is right here. God's glory beams out of that little manger!

Not only is Jesus the radiance of God's glory, but he is also *"the exact representation of [God's] being."* By coming in person, Jesus tells us exactly what God is like. He is furious with sin, absolutely intolerant of Satan and all his works and ways. He is absolutely here to declare war on the devil and all who are on his side. Yet he is full of endless mercy and endless patience for the fools and sinners who live here. He comes to give worth to you and to me. He hurts when his people hurt; he cries at the funerals of his friends. He had compassion on a widow who had to bury her son and then raised that son from the dead. He hurts when he sees people who are hungry, so he made food for five thousand of them, and he still makes food to feed you and me today. He has flesh and blood just like us. His tear ducts work and generate real salt tracks down his cheeks, just like yours. And he loves us so much that his heart can barely contain all the love that God crammed into every nook and cranny and valve and chamber. Look at Jesus and you see exactly who and how God is.

After telling you exactly who Jesus is, God now clearly says what he came to do: to purify you from your sins. You know that word, *purify?* Jesus is already pure, and now he says you are pure too. Do you look at yourself as pure? Or does your guilty conscious endlessly remind you of what a piece of trash you are? You are pure. He made purification *for* you! When you lay your head on the pillow tonight, you can say, "I am pure." Not on the basis of your own performance, but on the basis of *his* performance. He came to save you by purifying you from the evil that was polluting your life and would put you in hell. He provided purification as a gift, a Christmas gift, the gift of himself. He was made flesh to have something to be nailed onto a cross. You cannot nail a spirit to a cross; you cannot crucify a ghost. He has blood like us because without the shedding of blood there is no forgiveness.

After that incredible, amazing work was done, he went back to his Father and sat down at God's right hand. He is King Jesus, the Lord of the universe, who rules over all things. He inherited management of the cosmos and works for your good. What do you think of that? Do you believe that?

The final, mighty promise in this section says that he sustains this world. He controls every molecule, every atom, every subatomic particle, every wave. Everything in this universe is sustained and governed by his word. When he was physically here on earth, he could raise the dead, drive out demons, manufacture food out of nothing, and drive out illnesses. He did not stop doing that when he went back into heaven. He is still exerting his omnipotent power on your behalf to watch over all things. And when God says "all things," he means all things. Whatever is going on in your life right now is happening by the explicit permission of the God who loves you. He is moved by your tears, he knows your unspoken dreams, he knows your struggles, and he is acutely aware of your pain.

Maybe it just dawned on you as it did on me one day. Remember those questions we wish we could ask God, such as why are you letting these bad things happen to me? Here God gives us our answer. He has one goal and only one goal—getting you to the finish line, getting you home to heaven. He manages and sustains all things with that goal in mind. He has put everything on the line for the relationship he wants to have with you. It is his greatest desire.

Though you may feel as if you are stumbling along in the dark, your light has come. A child is born for you. Your Wonderful Counselor lived your life perfectly. Your Mighty God fought with Satan for you. Your Everlasting Father rescued you. Your Prince of Peace sustains you. Your Redeemer will come back for you. *That* is what he came to do for you. *That* is what he will do for you.

Chapter 5

Christic Is Born—So What?

Sociologists say that Christmas, which people think is supposed to be a day of magic, actually sees some of the worst abuse of alcohol. People drink heavily that day not because they are so happy, but because they are so sad. Christmas also shows spikes in domestic violence and abuse. Because of the stress and the unhappiness in people's lives, they take it out on one another. How can this be? Well, I think we set ourselves up by assuming that Christmas will automatically and magically pour happiness into the unhappy places in our hearts.

Maybe your family is arguing constantly and you are thinking, "At Christmas it will be better. We'll call a truce." Sometimes parents put enormous pressure on themselves to provide something magical for their children and overstretch themselves—and then the children whine about how they still were not given enough. Then there are the insecure hosts and hostesses, who put on a big event and worry if they have enough food or if the house is clean enough or decorated well enough. Or maybe you're worried about your job. How will you pay for all the stuff you are feeling pressured to buy?

Then there are widows at Christmastime, who look back at memories of happy Christmases and feel the intense sting of that empty chair all the more. People in the military hear the song "I'll be Home for Christmas," knowing the reality is they will be nowhere near home at what is supposed to be the most wonderful time of the year. This all has a way of diminishing the joy of the day, doesn't it? We all have a hunger for human relationships at this time of year. And we think there ought to be magic. Isn't Christmas supposed to make everything better? Instead, this magic time turns out to be a sad time.

The reality is that you are a broken sinner, and so are the other people you live with. No matter how hard you try, stuff happens; stuff breaks down. If you allow it to steal your joy, the devil will help you get so wound up that your time will be miserable. Maybe you will go to bed feeling embittered, and maybe you will say, "My Christmas was terrible. I've been cheated yet again." There is only one way out of this kind of trap, and that is to put Jesus right back in the middle of Christmas where he belongs. God has some thrilling—there is no other word for it—encouragement for you and me so that Satan will never again steal our joy. All the other stuff, whether business related, money related, presents related, materialism related, busyness related, or decoration and food related, will not be able to steal your joy if Christ is in the middle.

I know you know this, but we all get distracted by the demands on us and by the things we pile on ourselves to make the magic happen at Christmas. The irony is that the magic is already there. Just let the Bible tell you of the miracle of the incarnation. There is no more eloquent description of that incarnation I can think of than in the book of Hebrews. One of my favorite things about this book is that it bridges the Old and New Testaments. Some people have the idea that the New Testament completely replaced and made irrelevant the Old Testament. Actually, the New Testament fits into the Old like a hand in a glove; it completes everything.

That is why we have spent so much of our time in the Old Testament, so you too could see that Jesus was not ditching everything that came before but that he is the focal point of everything the Old Testament was leading up to. Hebrews ties the two together to show what an incredible, unified plan God has. He does not have two plans where one religion replaced another. There is one plan, one Savior, one faith, one path to be reconciled with God. Hebrews chapter 2 helps us understand the meaning of that plan, to see why it is crucially important both for your well-being right now and also for your eternity. Everything hinges on how you look at what happened in that barn at Bethlehem.

Since the children have flesh and blood, he too shared in their humanity so that by his death he might destroy him who holds the power of death—that is, the devil—and free those who all their lives were held in slavery by their fear of death. (Hebrews 2:14,15)

Christmas happened for one reason—our need. We, the children, were in a trap, boxed in by our own foolish rebellion against our Creator. Instead of giving up on us, that same Creator instead devised a rescue plan. His Son, Jesus, would come to earth, not to simply become *like* us but to *be* us. Jesus would share our humanness in every way, from conception to birth to adulthood. Jesus did not stop being God when he came to earth; he simply also became human. It reminds me of how in 1987 I became a father. I did not stop being who I was. It was just that now, in addition to everything else that I was before, I had a permanent new role that changed my identity. That is what Jesus did. He stayed God, *but he added our humanity to himself.*

With that new role, he took his human body and willingly put it on a cross where he had real nails driven through his real flesh and real blood spilled from his real veins. Hanging there, he put himself between you and the curse that has hung over the human race ever since the time of Adam and Eve. His real death, the payment for your sins, set you free from Satan and the power of death.

Even though Jesus crushed Satan's power, when we are honest with ourselves, fear of death still preys on our minds, doesn't it? Watching your own body disintegration is humiliating; seeing it happen in other people is heart-wrenching. Growing weaker makes you feel hopeless, as if all the good times are behind you. Not only is death bad, but the dying process is worse. We dread the experience. And after we die? Well, then you are held accountable for the way you have lived. That is what makes this really scary. Every one of us knows and feels and tastes guilt, which means we have a nagging fear that our meeting with The Man Upstairs is not going to be happy. That is slavery to fear.

But Christmas, the real Christmas, takes away that fear. It represents the moment at which the almighty, everlasting God himself came to this world in human flesh for our benefit. He made himself humble to save humble people—lowly, sinful, miserable people like us. He came to give us what we lacked with God. He came to give us objective, free, and unconditional approval and forgiveness for our sins. He came to let us claim his obedient, wonderful, and perfect life as though it were our own. And his death means we will never have to suffer death as a punishment. Instead, our death can now simply be our transition to go live with the everlasting Father.

For surely it is not angels he helps, but Abraham's descendants. For this reason he had to be made like his brothers in every way, in order that he might become a merciful and faithful high priest in service to God, and that he might make atonement for the sins of the people. (Hebrews 2:16,17)

In case you still did not believe all of this good news was for you personally, God says it a different way, "Look, this is not for the angels. Jesus came for real people with real needs." Jesus came to give you a hand-delivered message that we are his family. Jesus does not call you what you are by birth, which is convicted, condemned criminals. Instead, he calls you his brothers, his sisters, and his family, all because he likes you. He thought you were so valuable that it was worth going through a birth canal and being dropped into a donkey's feed box so he could share your struggles. He knew need and hunger. He knew exhaustion and sleeplessness. He is exquisitely familiar with psychological pain, emotional pain, and most certainly physical pain. Jesus can tell you straight up, right to your face, "I know what everything you are going through feels like. I have experienced it all."

Now, maybe some of the other parts of that passage did not make much sense. The children of Abraham knew all about sacrifices and priests and atonement, but today we do not really talk about those things at dinner parties. They are not part of our lives because when Christ came, he fulfilled the requirements and replaced some aspects of the Israelites' worship life. However, there is still a reason God put those things in the Bible for you to read. They give a clear, visual image of exactly what Jesus came to do. Back in Old Testament times, the high priest would present sacrifices on an altar. These animals were God's visual aids to teach people about the human condition and the way he interacts with us. As the people brought sacrifices for sin offerings, they knew it was not the animal's fault that there needed to be an offering. But in God's scheme of things, by allowing the animal to take the punishment, he taught the people it was okay to bring a replacement who would stand in and take the rap for you.

Because an animal is not of equal value to a human being, animal sacrifices were temporary and had to be repeated over and over. For your guilt, once a year, with great ceremony, the high priest would lay his hands on a goat who was about to be offered—literally, as though everyone could see the shame, guilt, and blame running right from the people of Israel, through the high priest's hands, onto the animal. Then because God wanted the people to see how bad sin is, the animal would be slaughtered, and blood would spray everywhere for all to see.

What a graphic image, don't you think? Kind of gross and disgusting? But the people who had witnessed these sacrifices immediately had a strong visual picture of what Jesus would do. What sets Jesus apart, however, is that he was both the high priest and the sacrifice simultaneously. He was the one who transferred the guilt from the people to the offering, and he was also the innocent victim who stepped in our place. That is why he was made like you, to be your friend and substitute so he could make the sacrifice for you and bring atonement to you.

That word *atonement* is beautiful. It means that one of Jesus' jobs is to make sure that you and God are *at one* again, no longer *at odds*. Jesus, by his life for you and death for you, made a final and complete payment for everything that put you at odds with God. This is mind blowing! Two thousand years before you were ever born your debts had all been prepaid. You are free from slavery. You are no longer enemies of God, no longer prisoners, no longer broken, no longer sinful fools, no longer objects of wrath. You are family.

Because he himself suffered when he was tempted, he is able to help those who are being tempted. (Hebrews 2:18)

Another job in Jesus' High Priestly duties is to be your advocate. You have someone who is still human in heaven. He bonded with us when he was born, and he kept his body when he ascended to heaven. Because he is human like us and had to struggle with Satan who attacked him at his moments of weakness, he has compassion for you when you struggle. He knows how hard it is to fight against Satan, not only when you are well rested and your savings account has a good balance but also when you have already taken a bunch of blows and one more comes. He has forgiveness for you when you fall. He has encouragement for you when you feel stupid and weak. He has love for you when you feel like nobody loves you. He boosts you up when you feel all alone. He has miracles still to give you. So when we ask for help, the Prince of Peace doesn't think us unworthy of his time; rather, he looks at you with great compassion and says, "I'm glad you're here. I have been where you've been, and I have help for you."

The other benefit of Jesus' being our advocate is that he does not wait for us to ask. As he sits next to God's right hand in heaven, he is constantly talking to the Father about you, asking him to be gentle with you, to be patient and kind, to give you the things that you need. God will never get tired of you or throw you away. The High Priest made the ultimate sacrifice for you.

These verses from the book of Hebrews bring great comfort, but you may still have some lingering frustrations. Maybe you have a Christmas to-do list and have not finished everything on it. Maybe you are worried about the big family event and how you will be judged. Maybe you are aching because you can't see your family. Maybe your family still acts in all kinds of dysfunctional ways. Maybe your own life is not under control and you're ashamed. Maybe you have regrets that no amount of alcohol can numb. All of those bad things may continue to happen. Leave them be. Let them slide away.

Celebrate the real joy of Christmas: the Son of God came to bring God's acceptance and pardon and forgiveness. If he forgives you, you can forgive yourself. If he says, "I love you," you can realize, "I am lovable." If he says, "I even like you," you can like yourself again.

All of that is true no matter what is going on in the rest of your life. What really matters is that God thinks that you are special and has declared you to be his child, now and forever. That relationship is something you can depend on no matter what is going on in the chaotic world that swirls around us. *That* is the real magic of Christmas.

Chapter 6

The Bonus Chapter

I have a confession. When our Time of Grace publishing team first suggested a Messiah book, the plans called for only five chapters. Well, as you are reading here, I have taken the liberty of adding a bonus chapter because, frankly, I can't get enough. I love what hearing the Christmas story and its meaning does for my faith, my confidence level, and my interactions with other people.

Maybe you have heard the story of Immanuel from the time you understood human language. Perhaps you came to know these things later in life. Possibly you are hearing the story for the very first time through this book. (If so, thank you for giving me the honor of sharing this amazing news with you!) I have heard the story of the Messiah every year since I was a child. That means I have heard it for 39 years now (wink).

I hope you will indulge me in one more chapter, to give me the opportunity to share one more little gem from Scripture. This last bit of encouragement comes from the apostle John, the "disciple whom Jesus loved." When John wrote these words, he was an old man, probably in his 80s or 90s. He did not feel the need to cover the *facts* of the stories Matthew and Luke had already written about—Joseph and Mary making the trek from Nazareth to Bethlehem, the astonishing story about the manger, the angels appearing to the shepherds, the Magi and the star in the sky, and wicked King Herod. Instead, he decided to use the energy in his aging hand for writing about the *significance* of everything he had seen. These words in the first chapter of his letter are some of the most extraordinary verses in the entire Bible, and I would like to savor them with you right now. We have had our meat and potatoes. Consider this our dessert.

The Word became flesh and made his dwelling among us. We have seen his glory, the glory of the One and Only, who came from the Father, full of grace and truth. (John 1:14)

"The Word" was John's little nickname for Jesus. Just as words share ideas and information and communicate emotion, Jesus is the way God passes his messages along to you. God took everything he wanted to tell you and made it into a human body. This does not mean that Isaiah and Micah's words, or any of the Old Testament words for that matter, are obsolete. Jesus simply, literally, fleshed them out. By fulfilling everything that had been said about the One who was to come, he showed them: "I am the one you've been waiting for. I am human like you. I am God with you. I am here."

His body was a hand-delivered love letter, the way God chose to tell you, "I love you still." He did this while we were still sinners. You can eat right, exercise, take care of your lawn, be nice to your neighbors, yet nothing you can do can make you holy enough for God, for whom nothing but absolute lifelong purity and sinlessness will suffice. So he did it for you. God himself came to earth as a human being, where Mary *"wrapped him in cloths and placed him in a manger, because there was no room for them in the inn"* (Luke 2:7). Just like that, "the Word" of God was made flesh. I don't actually understand this incredible mystery; I don't expect you to comprehend it either. What we can do, however, is believe God's Words and celebrate that God and humanity are now permanently fused together.

What also amazes me is that not only did he choose to become one of us, but he also chose to *live* with us. When the Bible says, *"he made his dwelling among us,"* the original Greek word literally means, "he pitched his tent." He camped here in the mud and the wallow like the rest of us. He subjected himself to every one of Satan's temptations, the same temptations that come at you and me every day. The only difference is he said no to all those temptations to compensate for the millions of times we said yes. He came to live the holy life Adam and Eve and all of us were supposed to have lived, but failed. He came as your personal substitute and did it for you perfectly for about 33 years. He came and opened up his heart to be ripped to pieces by sharing in the sufferings that all people go through. He came to hold little children in his lap. He came to touch people who were suffering, the people who were crippled, the deaf and blind, those who were grieving and crying.

That Jesus came camping with us for a little while but then went back to his Father in heaven is a good reminder that we are only camping here too. We live in temporary tents, waiting for him to come back for us, the same way the Israelites waited for his first grand entrance. Sometimes we wait patiently, enjoying this good gift of people and family and creation that God gave us. Sometimes we wait impatiently, complaining and groaning with the pain and hurt in this world. But we wait, knowing that just as God chose the right time to send the Word to be born, God will wait until just the right time to call us to our permanent home.

Let me tell you, I cannot wait for my permanent room in God's mansion. In heaven, God tells us, *"The city does not need the sun or the moon to shine on it, for the glory of God gives it light, and the Lamb is its lamp"* (Revelation 21:23). Isn't that amazing? God's glory is so bright that we will never need the sun again. He also knew we would not be able to wrap our brains around that concept, so he gave us a taste.

The "glory of the Lord" appears all through the Old Testament as an intense bright fire and cloud in which God let people see that he was advancing his plan of salvation in a significant way. For Abraham, God appeared as a smoking firepot to confirm his promise that Abraham would be the father of God's nation. In a bush that would not burn up, Moses heard God's commission to bring liberation to the slaves in Egypt.

In a pillar of cloud and fire, God showed the Israelite people that he was both protecting them from the chariots of Egypt and leading and guiding them where to go next. When Solomon dedicated the temple, as his last prayer rolled up to heaven, suddenly the bright cloud appeared. Everyone saw it go into the temple and hover over the ark of the covenant to show that their God was among them and he had come to help them.

That glory was not only for people in the Old Testament. John says, *"We have seen his glory."* When Jesus was crucified, the curtain of the temple ripped in two and the most holy place behind the veil was open for all to see. The bright cloud was gone, because Christ is the final, ultimate glory of the Lord. The disciples saw that glory when he changed water into wine. Once, on a mountainside, three specially chosen disciples got to see Jesus as he is now, radiant and transfigured, shining in holiness and power. This is the real thing. Our God really did come to earth. We have seen the glory of the Word made flesh, who tented with us for a while.

Jesus came to earth with his arms full of presents. John says that Christ is full of *grace* and *truth*, two things in terribly short supply on earth and two things that you desperately need. He knew you would wonder, "What am I doing here? What's the purpose of my life? Can I go back to God when I have messed up? Can I find God when I have been blindly stumbling around? I have had streaks of major stupidity in my life. Can I ever crawl back? And how can I ever expect God to *listen* to little, foolish, sinful me? What makes me think I can pray to him and expect any kind of a hearing?"

That's why Jesus came full of grace, which tells you that God loves you because *he wants* to love you, because *he chooses* to love you, no matter what you have done. For the rest of your life, you can look at the Word made flesh and know you have a place to go when you are broken, when you are miserable, when you are confused, when you are hurt. When you start to think you are all alone, go back to Bethlehem's manger and see God is not angry with you at all. Immanuel is smiling at you and saying, "I choose to treat you in grace, unconditionally. I forgive you. Now go and live for me."

Do you see why this is so important? When you want things to be better in your life—more love, more security, less conflict, more strength—the starting point is not in your own messy life *but in God's grace!*

Jesus Christ is full of grace, so full that you can never exhaust it. He knows you are weak and doesn't despise you. He knows you are tired, knows your fears, and knows your insecurities. The power comes from him; the love comes from him; the wisdom and vision also come from him. From him come patience and stamina, daily bread and hope, kind friends and words of encouragement.

Jesus is also full of *truth*. Do you see why that is so important? Every day we are barraged by messages that originate with the evil one, messages that are lies. From hell come the insults that seek to beat you down. Loser! Worthless! Ugly! Failure! The Christmas story tells you the truth, that Jesus thought you so valuable that he emptied himself of his heavenly glory and comforts, took on the very nature of a servant, and made himself obedient to death. Why? *For you!* That's the truth.

The first chapter of John's gospel says that to all who believe in his name he gave the right to be called the children of God. That's the truth! Because of Christmas, because of the miracle of the incarnation, you are loved, you are forgiven, you are adopted into your new family. He came to earth like a sweet little gift, wrapped in strips of cloth. His poverty has become your wealth.

You may fear that this coming Christmas will be a bust. You can't afford to give the kind of presents that you would like, and you know that nobody's going to break the bank giving you anything. No matter. It's not you who is "giving Christmas" to members of your family. It is Christ who gives you things that matter: the gift of peace with the Father and the gift of eternal life with him.

Oh, come, let us adore him!

Study Guides

(For printable study guides, please visit the Time of Grace website at timeofgrace.org.)

Chapter 1
Who Will He Be?

A personal look
Isaiah 7:9-14

- God made things clear for Ahaz: *"If you do not stand firm in your faith, you will not stand at all."* The same goes for you too. Does this encourage you or scare you for the next time a seemingly insurmountable challenge stands before you?

- Have you ever asked God for a sign? How did he answer that request?

- Ahaz wouldn't ask God for a sign, so Isaiah said, *"Therefore the Lord himself will give you a sign: The virgin will be with child and will give birth to a son, and will call him Immanuel."* God gave the greatest promise ever: divine help is coming. How does God's sign give hope to you in the middle of your gloomiest days?

Isaiah 59:9-15; 60:1,2

- What in your life is dark right now, whether caused by your own actions, actions of others, or simply life in general?

- How can knowing that the glory of the Lord has already come and is already over you change your perspective of your troubles?

What else does God say about this?
The following passages explain more about who this Messiah is. What does each one say about Jesus?
Luke 24:39
2 Peter 1:17
1 John 5:20

Prayer

Dear Lord Jesus, you truly are Immanuel; you are God with us. How wonderful that you—Almighty God from all eternity—came in person to our world, to my world, to bring rescue to me and to all people. How can we thank you enough for being willing to subject yourself to such humility to be able to lift us up so high? Take away my gloom and darkness. Remind me that your light is over and around and on me. Thank you, Lord, for being my Messiah, God with me, true God, true man. Amen.

Chapter 2
What Kind of Welcome Does He Deserve?

A personal look
Matthew 2:1-12

- What does the prominent role of the Magi in this story tell you about who is part of God's family?

- Jesus left the riches of heaven to be born into poverty, and yet Jesus was welcomed like a king. How does this affect your perspective and priorities?

- Contemplate the risks these Magi took to meet Jesus and their behavior once they met him. Does this shed new light on this familiar story? How can this change the way you welcome Jesus?

Matthew 3:1-3,5,6; Luke 3:7,8,10-14

- What in your life needs to be straightened, filled in, or leveled down? What does "be repenting" look like in your life?

- You do not bear fruit to earn God's favor. Instead, you do good things because you are already part of God's family. What change does this have on your attitude toward serving others?

What else does God say about this?
Dig deeper into your Bible by reading more about these truths and see how you can give Jesus the welcome he deserves.

- How can John 11:25,26 help remind you that it is all about Jesus?

- What do these three passages tell you about how to live your life of faith?
  Joshua 1:9
  Psalm 31:24
  2 Corinthians 3:12

- The Magi sought out Jesus. How can you do the same from where you live? Read Deuteronomy 4:29; Psalm 9:10; Psalm 95:6,7; and Revelation 4:10,11.

Prayer

Lord Jesus, we come before you and give you our worship and praise that you became human flesh for us to live our lives, die our deaths, and to open up your home to be our home. Thank you for the example of the Magi, who help us see that we can seek you too, to give you our hearts. May we also honor you with our treasures, with gifts fit for a King. Be thrilled and pleased in your heart to receive our gifts, as we produce fruit in keeping with repentance. We love you and pray in your holy name. Amen.

Chapter 3
Where Will He Come From?

A personal look
Micah 4:10-12; 5:1-5
- How have you been tempted, like the people of Israel, to rely on your own strength?

- Micah points out that it would get bad for the people of God, but even then, hundreds of years before his birth, God points them and us to Christ. What can get in the way of seeing Christ when things look bleak?

- In this reading, Jesus is depicted as a shepherd. Shepherds guide, feed, and protect their sheep. List ways our Shepherd is guiding, feeding, and protecting you now.

- About 750 years passed between the time God promised that the Savior would come from Bethlehem until the time the Messiah arrived. What does this tell you about how God guides world events and your life's events?

What else does God say about this?
Dig deeper into your Bible by reading more about these truths and find out why keeping even small promises is a big deal to our God.
- What do these passages say about God and his promises?
  1 Samuel 15:29
  Psalm 105:8

- The next time things look bleak, how will these passages remind you that the Light of the World is here?
  Psalm 34:10

Romans 8:32
2 Peter 3:9

- What else does the Bible tells us about our Shepherd? Read Psalm 23:1; 1 Peter 2:25; and 1 Peter 5:4.

- The first time Jesus came to earth, he was born in Bethlehem. When he comes back, where will he come from? Read John 14:2,3; John 17:5; and Ephesians 4:10.

Prayer
Lord Jesus, we thank you for coming to our world. We thank you for coming even to such a small and insignificant place as little Bethlehem. And yet, the smallness of your birthplace is dwarfed by the vastness of the wonderful thing that you came to bring. Even though your prophets announced judgment upon human sin, you came to bring forgiveness for human sin. Right now we celebrate that gift as our most wonderful Christmas present and thank and praise you for shepherding us through this world. Hear us, Jesus, for we pray in your name. Amen.

Chapter 4
What Did He Come to Do?

A personal look
Isaiah 9:1-7

- For those walking in darkness, Jesus shines light on every situation. How has he lit the way for you to no longer live in darkness? How are you able to use your experience to help show others the Light?

- Even as death stalks us all, how does Jesus enlarge and increase your joy?

- The Messiah comes to end our slavery to sin, to stop war and all the ravages of sin, to be worshiped as God, to bring everlasting peace for our souls, and to restore all created things to their Creator. List some of the ways Jesus has been your
  Wonderful Counselor
  Mighty God
  Everlasting Father
  Prince of Peace

Hebrews 1:1-3

- Do you ever feel like nobody understands what you're going through? How does knowing that Jesus sustains all things change your perspective?

- Because of Jesus, you are pure. Write down a list of things that drag you down and make you feel as if you aren't valuable. Then cross it off and write "PAID IN FULL" over it.

- What things in your life right now make you ask, "Why is this happening to me?" Knowing that God's only goal is to get you home with him forever, how can you take a fresh look at your situation?

What else does God say about this?
You can dig deeper into your Bible by reading more about what God said he sent Jesus to do.
- After reading these passages, list what Jesus came to do and how it applies to your life.
Isaiah 53:5
John 8:34,36
John 14:27
Romans 8:1
2 Corinthians 5:17-19
Colossians 3:15
Hebrews 12:2
1 John 1:7

Prayer
Lord, Prince of Peace, bring peace to every home that hears the wonderful news that you have come to be our Wonderful Counselor, Mighty God, Everlasting Father, and Prince of Peace. Thank you for purifying us and showing the Father to us. Help us reflect your glory to everyone we meet. Lord Jesus, we pray in your holy name. Amen.

Chapter 5
Christ Is Born—So What?

A personal look
Hebrews 2:14-18

- Sometimes Christmas can be a sad time if we focus on ourselves and our lives. What in your life right now causes you to lose joy at Christmas?

- Read Hebrews 2:17,18. The coming of Jesus means we have a High Priest who brings us atonement with God. He is our advocate. Jesus was tempted just as we are, so he understands our weaknesses. How does this change what Christmas means for you?

- Christmas is about Jesus. God took on humanity to take away the fear of death because he took away eternal death for all who believe in him. Which people in your life do not know this astonishing news? How will you share it with them?

What else does God say about this?
Dig deeper to see just how Christmas changes your life.

- Christmas = Jesus! How will you help your own home stay focused on Jesus? Read John 18:36,37 and 1 Corinthians 15:56,57.

- After looking at Jesus' life, which of your attitudes need to change? See Philippians 2:5-8.

- Think of the ways your enemy tries to tempt you and tell you that you are still in slavery. How does Jesus help you through this? Read Mark 9:23,24 and 1 Corinthians 10:13.

- You are in a state of at-one-ment with your God. How can you remember that "it is finished" every day? Read Romans 8:1 and Hebrews 7:26,27.

Prayer

Dear Lord, thank you today that in spite of all my imperfections, you have called me perfect—perfectly forgiven, perfectly loved, perfectly immortal, perfect in the image of your Son, Jesus. Thank you for the perfect Christmas gift, which makes up for all the imperfections in my life. Help me deal with all the disappointments in my life by remembering that I don't have to put pressure on myself to clean myself up for you. You love me already as I am, and I have a Savior who forgives me. Help me show that same kindness and patience to other people. Because of you, every day is Christmas, and I thank you for it in Jesus' name. Amen.

Chapter 6
The Bonus Chapter

A personal look
John 1:14

- What message from "the Word" do you most need to hear right now?

- Have you ever wondered if you can go back to God when you have messed up? How does grace give you the answer?

- How have you seen the grace of God in your life?

What else does God say about this?
Dig deeper to see how Messiah changes everything.

- How does your world look from your tent? Does your perspective change when you consider that you are only camping here? See 2 Corinthians 5:1-4.

- How has Jesus transformed your life? See Ephesians 2:1-7.

Prayer
Dear Jesus, we bow before you, humbly, happily, because you are the Word. Without you, we would have no idea who the Father is and what his plan is for us. Thank you for coming in a human body to show us God's love, his mercy, his plan to bring us back to him forever. How amazing that we get to see the glory of God in you, to let us know that God likes us and loves us. You are Immanuel. You are "God with us." And someday, we will be with you. Until then, keep interceding for us from your throne in heaven. In your dear name we pray. Amen.

Notes:

Notes:

_____

_____

_____

_____

_____

_____

_____

_____

_____

_____

_____

_____

_____

_____

_____

_____

_____

_____

_____

_____

Notes:

Notes:

Notes:

.